From Data Structures
to Patterns

From Data Structures to Patterns

Darrel Ince

First published 2000
MACMILLAN PRESS LTD
Houndmills, Basingstoke, Hampshire RG21 6XS
and London
Companies and representatives throughout the world.

ISBN 0-333-77444-2

A catalogue record for this book is available
from the British Library.

This book is printed on paper suitable for recycling and
made from fully managed and sustained forest sources.

10   9   8   7   6   5   4   3   2   1
09   08   07   06   05   04   03   02   01   00

Printed in Great Britain by Antony Rowe Ltd, Chippenham, Wiltshire.

Contents

Preface

During the Summer of 1997 I suffered a sporting injury which meant that
I had to lie horizontally for fourteen weeks. The period of enforced rest
enabled me to plan this book. For a number of months before sustaining
this injury I had become increasingly concerned that the current way we
approached data was at variance with the facilities offered by modern
object-oriented programming languages such as Java and C++. This is
often evidenced by the fact that many current textbooks are really
conversions of existing books written for procedural languages such as C,
with perhaps some inclination towards the use of data hiding.

A typical course on data is usually given the title: *Data Structures and
Abstract Data Types*. Such a course concentrates on the algorithms which
describe how to implement abstract data types such as sets, sequences and
tables together with supporting material on topics such as sorting. While
this material is valuable it gives rise to a problem that bothered me.

This problem was that such courses are at variance with the fact that
most object-oriented languages offer excellent facilities for entities such as
sets and sequences and relieve the programmer of the burden of
implementing small data collections; for example, the JGL library freely
distributed by *ObjectSpace*, the Java 2 collection classes and the STL library
for C++ should mean that object-oriented programmers really do not
need to develop basic data type code any more.

While existing books offer valuable teaching on the strategies required
for algorithm development—strategies which, for example, give rise to
greedy algorithms and divide-and-conquer algorithms—they do have a
missing dimension; one which has become important over the last five
years as object-oriented technology has increasingly impinged on the
computing curriculum. This missing dimension is that there is little
material on how to design large abstract data types which may contain
many small data types. Modern computer systems do not just contain a
single set or a sequence but will be made up of a variety of abstract data
types combined using aggregation and inheritance. Because of this I
decided to devote a considerable amount of teaching to this topic in the
middle of the book.

The last third of the book is devoted to patterns, primarily those
concerned with data storage. During the last few years a number of
researchers have pointed out that modern object-oriented systems contain
certain common patterns which support reuse and extension. Patterns
have been so enthusiastically taken up by industrial developers that a book

on data such as this one would be flawed if it didn't contain material on this topic.

In writing this book I have assumed that the reader has a knowledge of the Java programming language gained from an introductory programming course in the language; typically a course offered in the first year of a degree.

This book represents a transition between the type of data structures book represented by Sedgwick's *Algorithms* and the sort of reusable software books that I would imagine would be written now and between 2005. Data structure and abstract data type books are oriented towards a student body whose members leave university to work in industry or to do research (an increasingly small minority). In truth, if you are in the second category, then this is not the book for you. However, if you are in the former category, then I hope you will find my treatment a valuable introduction to the sort of work that you will be carrying out in the next decade.

Darrel Ince
Milton Keynes, 2000

Introduction

This chapter:
- Describes the central role of data in a system.
- Outlines the contents of the remainder of the book.
- Introduces a number of collections.
- Shows how data that supports complex applications can be split into smaller collections of data.

This chapter is purely introductory and sets down the main themes in the first third of the book.

1.1 Introduction

Computer systems consist of two elements: data and programs. Each is important; however, the choice of data—how it is structured and how it is accessed—can make the difference between extreme slowness or lightning speed. This book is about data, after reading it you will be equipped with the techniques necessary to design the data component of a system, choose between competing designs and be able to develop the program code that interacts with the data component.

1.2 An example

In order to describe the important concepts detailed in the first half of this book an example is in order; it involves the Internet. The Internet is a collection of computer networks which are connected together using a variety of media including communication lines, infrared waves and wireless waves. It is massive, with hundreds of thousands of computers connected together. A typical collection of data that is used in the Internet is shown in Figure 1.1.

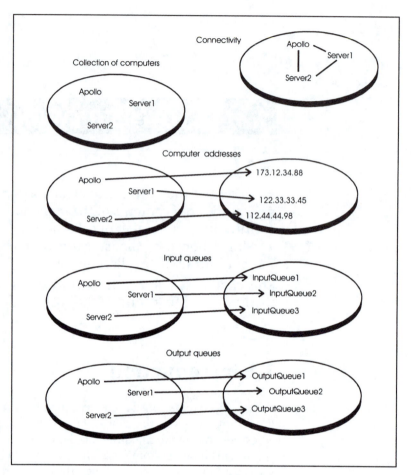

Figure 1.1
Data used in a
messaging
system

There are a number of components that make up this collection of data. First, there is a collection of queues. They contain messages that are to be sent from one computer to another. These queues are partitioned into two types: input queues and output queues. An input queue contains messages that have been received by a computer on the Internet and are either awaiting processing by the computer associated with the queue, or are awaiting transmission to other computers on the Internet. An output queue contains messages that are to be sent to other computers on the Internet. In this example each computer is associated with one input queue and one output queue.

A second component of this messaging system is a collection of computers with links to other computers. This collection contains a linked set of computer names with no duplication. When the software that is associated with the messaging system removes a message from the output queue of a computer it finds out whether it is meant for one of the computers which it is directly connected to. If it is then it sends it to that computer; however, if it isn't meant for the destination computer then it is sent to another computer that has the function of forwarding the message to other parts of the Internet.

The third component of the data is the collection which associates each computer with its address. In Figure 1.1 this address is expressed in what is known as dotted quad notation: four integers separated by dots which uniquely determine the address of a computer on the Internet.

1.3 Some concepts

The example in the previous section illustrates a number of important points about data. First, and probably the most obvious, is the fact that one can view the data in a system at a high level. Figure 1.1 does not include any details about how the data is implemented; there is, for example, no indication whether the message queues are implemented using an array or via pointers. What one sees in Figure 1.1 is a high level data design.

The second important point is that each of the components of the data—the message queues, individual messages and the collection of connected computers—have different properties. For example, the message queues are ordered on the time at which a message arrives at the computer and the collection of connected computers contains no duplicates and is unordered.

The third point to make about the example is that Figure 1.1 shows a collection which is made up from smaller collections: queues, a set of computers, a set of computers with their connections and a collection of computers with their Internet addresses.

The fourth point is that the collection of data is associated with a number of operations. Some of these are shown below:

▸ An operation that determines which message to process in an input queue, removes the message, processes it and then deposits it in an output queue.

▸ An operation which adds a new computer to the collection of computers. This occurs when a new computer is added.

▸ An operation which removes an exiting computer from the collection of computers. This occurs when a computer is retired.

▸ An operation which moves a collection of messages from an input queue to an output queue when the computer discovers a collection of messages is destined for another computer.

These operations will be implemented in program code.

The fifth point is that the operations on the overall collection of data can be split up into operations on individual collections. For example, the operation which examines an input queue, removes a message, processes it and then deposits it into an output queue, can be split up into the following operations:

▶ An operation which takes a message from an input queue.

▶ An operation which determines whether the message is meant for the home computer.

▶ An operation which determines whether the message is meant for a connected computer.

▶ An operation which sends the message either to a known destination computer which it is directly connected to or to a forwarding computer which can then send it on to its final destination.

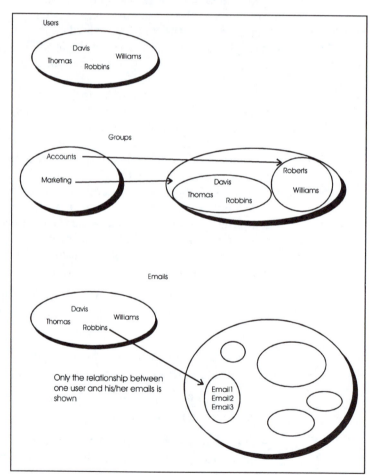

Figure 1.2 An architecture for an email system

SELF TEST QUESTION 1

The collection of data shown in Figure 1.2 describes the data architecture of a program which administers the storage of emails. The figure shows a collection of users, the emails they have received and also a collection of users split into a number of groups which correspond to departments in their workplace. Write down a number of operations which such a system might be associated with. The answer to this question and all other self test questions can be found in the Appendix.

SELF TEST QUESTION 2

Detail some of the primitive operations which are executed when the fifth operation detailed in the answer to the self test question above is executed.

1.4 The collections

In the previous example there are a number of different collections of data; at this stage in the book it is worth giving them a name. A collection of data in which there are no duplicates is known as a set, the collection of connected computers in Figure 1.1 is an example of a set. A collection of data where there is some ordering inherent in the collection is known as a sequence, the queues which hold messages in Figure 1.1 are all examples of sequences. A collection of data which reflects some connection between two different collections is known as a table or a map. In Figure 1.1 there are three examples of maps: there is the association between computers and input queues, the association between computers and output queues and the association between the symbolic name of a computer and its address.

1.5 Another example

Figure 1.3 represents another networking application. It shows the topology of a computer network: the individual computers in a network and the connections between each computer. Such a collection of data is used to determine the route taken by a message that traverses the Internet.

This data forms part of a routing system based on a concept known as a hop. Each computer that a message passes through is a single hop. A simple algorithm for determining the route through a network is one which finds the minimum distance between the computer sending the message and the computer receiving the message—the distance expressed as the number of hops. The programming required for minimum hop routing is simple. However, it is not the ideal way of determining the fastest path through a network. The most important factor it ignores is the fact that traffic at a particular computer could be very heavy and the message might need to wait for a long time before it gets passed on to another computer.

In order to be able to use more sophisticated algorithms more information is required which relates traffic conditions at a particular computer to that computer.

SELF TEST QUESTION 3

What data type would you use to relate traffic conditions to a computer?

The example described here has all the features of the previous example:

▶ It is a view of the data at a high level, no implementation details are described.

▶ It consists of different components with different properties.

▶ The whole collection is made up from smaller collections.

▶ Operations can be defined on the overall collection; for example, an important operation is that of determining the fastest route through the network between two computers.

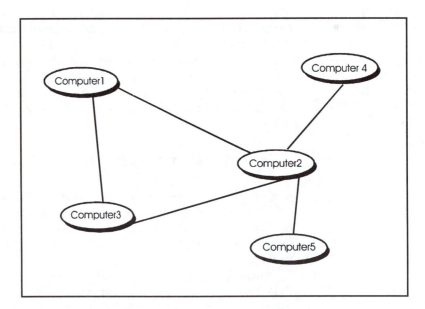

Figure 1.3
Router Data

High-level operations such as the one above can be decomposed into operations on the sub-components; for example, determining the quickest route will involve accessing both the data collection representing the hops and also the data which holds the traffic conditions data.

SELF TEST QUESTION 4

Can you list some of the operations that are associated with the data shown in Figure 1.3?

Before leaving this example it is worth saying that another different collection of data has been introduced. The collection of data that relates a computer to a number of other computers is known as a graph. This is a collection which relates an entity such as a computer to a collection of one or more other entities. Graphs will be described along with the other data types introduced here in later chapters of the book.

1.6 About this book

This book is about data. Chapter 2 continues the theme elucidated by this chapter. It describes the concept of an abstract data type: a view of a collection of data that is unencumbered by implementation details. It then describes the relationship between an abstract data type and the concrete data structures that can be found in a programming language. The chapter concludes by looking at the abstract data types: set, sequence, map and graph briefly introduced in this chapter.

Chapter 3 is a discussion of the implementation of abstract data types and how it involves making trade-offs between programming complexity, speed, memory requirements and degree of applicability.

Chapters 4 to 6 describe the techniques used to implement some of the main abstract data types introduced in the book. Each chapter is devoted to a particular abstract data type and provides Java code for a number of different implementations.

Chapter 7 represents a transition from the first half of the book. This chapter describes how large collections such as the three presented in this chapter can be built up using two techniques: aggregation and inheritance.

Chapter 8 represents a change of direction. Chapters 4 to 6 describe individual data types in terms of how to program them. Over the last five years a number of high quality data structure libraries have been developed for object-oriented languages such as C++ and Java. This means that much of the implementation of small collections of data such as the set has been taken away from the programmer. This chapter describes two modern data structure packages for Java: one is known as the Java Generic Library (JGL) and the other is the package of collection classes used in Java 2.

Chapter 9 describes a number of examples of large data implementations. Most of them use JGL or the Java 2 collections. Chapter 10 describes how aggregation and inheritance can be used to implement an important collection known as a graph.

Chapter 11 introduces the concept of a pattern. This is a combination of classes which occur time and time again in good system designs. Such patterns can be catalogued and reused time and time again. The chapter describes three simple patterns.

Chapter 12 describes a major pattern which lies at the heart of a mailing list administration system. The pattern is known as the *Composite* pattern. It is used to describe collections which are split it into sub-collections which, in turn are split into further sub-sub-collections etc. Finally, Chapter 13 looks at a number of further patterns associated with the mailing list administration system detailed in Chapter 12.

CHAPTER SUMMARY

▶ Collections of data can be split into smaller collections.

▶ There are a number of collection types that have distinct properties.

▶ A high-level operation on data can be split into a number of lower level operations.

Abstract Data Types

This chapter:

▶ Introduces the central idea of an abstract data type.
▶ Describes the four basic abstract data types: set, map, graph and sequence.
▶ Outlines the relationship between an abstract data type and its implementation.

This chapter acts as a prelude to the next four chapters in that it discusses central concepts which will be referred to time and time again in those chapters.

2.1 Introduction

An abstract data type is data identified by its operations. As an example consider Figure 2.1. This shows the data involved in part of an operating system known as a block manager. Files in a computer operating system are stored as collections of data known as blocks consisting of a collection of bytes. Each file stored in the operating system is uniquely identified by a collection of block numbers. During the execution of the operating system files will be created and deleted; when a file is created the blocks from which it is constructed are taken from a collection of free blocks labelled *Free blocks* in Figure 2.1.

When a user deletes a file the blocks which make up that file are added to a queue of blocks waiting to be added to the collection of free blocks. This queue is shown in the bottom half of Figure 2.1. When the operating system has little else to do it examines the queue of blocks and removes the head of the queue and places all the blocks there in the collection of free blocks.

The example contains two of the main abstract data types that you will need when constructing serious software systems:

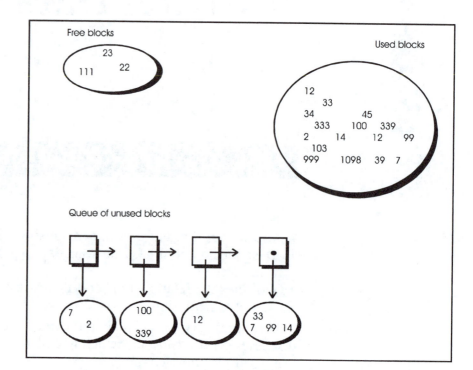

Figure 2.1 A block handler

▶ *The set.* A set is a collection of data in which no duplication is allowed. In the operating system example above the collection of free blocks is an example of a set since there is no duplication.

▶ *The sequence.* A sequence is a collection of data which is ordered. The ordering may be based on the values in the sequence—for example, the sequence may consist of integers in ascending order—or it may be ordered in time; for example, in a queue the items may be stored in the order in which they are added. In Figure 2.1 the queue of collections of blocks is an example of a sequence.

It is worth pointing out that not only do abstract data types contain simple items of data such as strings and integers but also contain instances of other abstract data types. A good example of this is shown in Figure 2.1. Here the queue of unused blocks is a sequence whose elements are themselves sets.

Each of the instances of abstract data types in this example are associated with operations; for example, the queue of blocks waiting to be unallocated is associated with operations which add a collection of blocks and remove a collection of blocks.

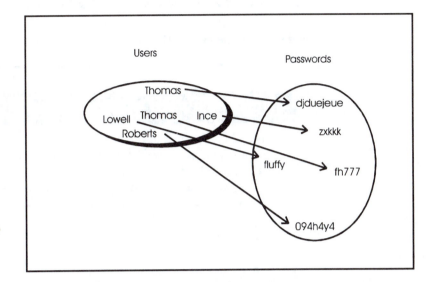

Figure 2.2 A map used to store user passwords

SELF TEST QUESTION 1

Can you write down some more high-level operations which are associated with the data type shown in Figure 2.1?

These, then, are three of the operations that can affect the collection of free blocks, used blocks and the queue of blocks. They all correspond to actions that occur during the execution of the operating system; for example, blocks would be taken from the collection of free blocks when a file is created.

The example described in the self test question above illustrates a number of important points about abstract data types:

▶ There are a number of basic abstract data types from which larger data types can be constructed.

▶ An abstract data type is associated with a number of operations.

▶ Operations on abstract data types will correspond to operations in the real world.

In order to illustrate these points consider another example associated with an operating system.

Figure 2.2 shows the use of the map abstract data type for storing user identities and associated passwords in an operating system. A typical operation that would be associated with this data type would be one in which a new user/password entry is added to the data type.

SELF TEST QUESTION 2

Can you write down some more operations which are associated with the data type in Figure 2.2?

SELF TEST QUESTION 3

The operations detailed in the previous question are low-level operations on the individual data type. What high-level operations do these take part in? For each of the operations described in the previous question can you write down what action in the operating system the operation represents.

2.2 Operations

As we have already stated abstract data types are associated with operations. There are three types of operation:

▶ Operations which extract part of the data from an instance of an abstract data type and returns with some information about the instance. An example of this type of operation would be one which accessed a sequence and returned with the number of items currently in the sequence. Another example is an operation which checks whether a particular item of data is in a set; if it is, then it returns with a true value, otherwise it returns with a false value. This category of operation does not affect the data which it accesses.

▶ Operations which update an instance of an abstract data type with some data. An operation which adds a collection of blocks to the end of the queue of blocks in Figure 2.1 is an example of this type of operation.

▶ Operations which carry out some updating and also return with some value. An operation which removes the item at the front of the queue of blocks and returns with that item falls into this category.

SELF TEST QUESTION 4

The queues of orders in a purchasing system is modelled by a sequence of orders. What updating operations would be associated with this data type?

Can you think of any operations which retrieve some data from the queue detailed in the previous self test question?

2.3 Some basic abstract data types

In this section a number of basic abstract data types are described. Each of them has already been briefly introduced in the previous section. This section provides the details; later chapters will describe their implementation.

2.3.1 The set

A set is a collection of items each of which is unique. Examples of sets are:

▶ The set of employees in a system for paying staff working for a company.

▶ The set of computers in a network.

▶ The set of planes which have landed at an airport in an air-traffic control system.

▶ The set of words stored in the spelling checker of a word processor.

There are a number of operations associated with sets:

▶ *member*. This checks whether a particular item of data is contained in a set. It returns true if the item is found and false if it is not found.

▶ *add*. This updates a set by adding an item to it.

▶ *remove*. The opposite of addition. An item which is in the set is removed.

▶ *size*. This operation returns with the number of items in the set.

▶ *union*. This operation takes two sets and forms a set by collecting together all their members. Any duplicates are ignored. So, for example, if one set contained the integers 5, 7, 9 and 99 and the second set contained the integers 3, 5, 10 and 56, then the union of these sets is the set 3, 5, 7, 9, 10, 56 and 99.

▶ *intersection*. This operation takes two sets and forms the set which contains all the common members of each set. For example, if the first set contains the integers 1, 3, 5 and 66, and the second set contains the integers 3, 7, 88 and 99, then the intersection of these sets is the set containing only the integer 3.

Chapter 4 describes a number of implementations of sets. A set is used when there is a requirement to store unique items in a collection and to carry out operations such as finding whether an item is contained in a set.

SELF TEST QUESTION 6

Which of the following data would be stored in a set?

▶ The collection of different computers which are sold by a computer warehouse.

▶ The collection of staff who have been with a company for more than ten years.

▶ The collection of data which links an employee in a company to his or her salary.

▶ The collection of data which links an item of stock to the quantity of the item currently stored in a warehouse.

2.3.2 The sequence

A sequence is a collection of data which is ordered in some way. Sequences proliferate in computing. For example, in a communications system the computers that make up the system are associated with queues which contain messages that are awaiting processing from other computers. The ordering criterion that determines how data is added into a sequence can depend on time, the content of the data or some other data. A queue is an example of a sequence where the ordering is based on time: the items that are added to the queue are placed in a position (the end) which depends on when the items were added. A queue of purchase orders being processed by an ordering system, which is ordered on the importance of the customer who has placed the order, is an example of a sequence which is ordered on other data: the priority of customers.

There are a number of common operations associated with sequences:

▶ *add*. This adds an item to a sequence. The position where the item is added depends on the ordering criterion used for the sequence.

▶ *removeHead*. This removes the item at the head of the sequence.

▶ *removeItem*. This removes an item which could be in any position within the sequence. The item is identified by some unique property. For example, in a sequence of purchase orders the item would be identified by its purchase number.

▶ *size*. This returns with the number of items within the sequence.

▶ *inSequence*. This returns with a Boolean true value if an item is found in the sequence, and false otherwise.

SELF TEST QUESTION 7

Which abstract data types would you use for the following collections of data:

▶ The cars which are owned by a car hire company.

▶ The queue of messages which are to be processed by a computer in a telecommunications system.

▶ The collection of computers which make up a computer network.

2.3.3 The map

A map is a collection of data which consists of pairs. The first item of the pair is related to the second item of the pair through some rule. For example, Figure 2.3 shows a map which relates an employee's work number to their name.

Each item in the map contains a pair which is the name of the employee and the employee's work number. In a map one of the items in a pair will be unique. This item is known as the key. In the map shown in Figure 2.3 the key is the works number.

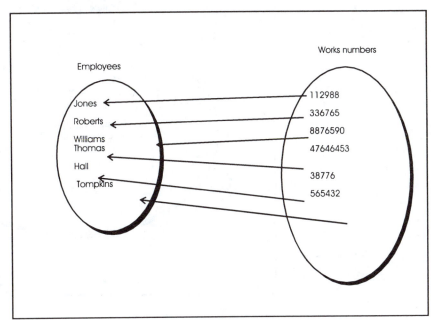

Figure 2.3 A map

Remember that a map represents an association between two sets. For example, the map shown in Figure 2.3 represents an association between a set of employees and a set of integers which represent the works numbers. Maps are used to implement collections of data where there is a requirement for values in one set to be returned based on the key values in another set. For example, an air-traffic control system might use a map to associate a particular flight with its geographical position along its flight path.

There are a number of common operations associated with maps:

▶ *size*. This returns with the number of pairs in the map.

▶ *inMap*. This returns true if a particular pair is in the map. The pair is identified by its key.

▶ *add*. This adds a pair to a map.

▶ *find*. This returns with an element in a map which is paired with a particular key element.

▶ *remove*. This removes a pair from a map. The pair is identified by its key.

SELF TEST QUESTION 8

Which abstract data types would you use for the following collections of data:

▶ The staff employed by a company.

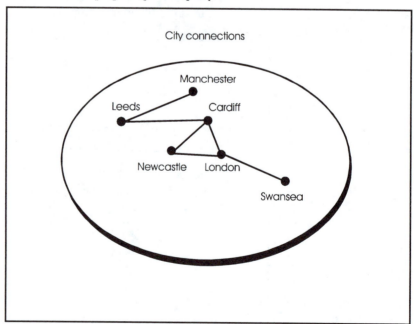

Figure 2.4 A graph

▸ The cars waiting in a queue at a roundabout.

▸ The data which associates a car with the employee in a company who uses it.

▸ The collection of data which represents the destination of lorries which are currently out on the road working for a haulage firm.

2.3.4 The graph

A graph is a data type which relates a number of items of data together where one item is related to a number of other items. This is in contrast to a map where the association is between one item and another item. An example of a graph is shown in Figure 2.4. It relates towns and cities to the roads that connect them together. Here the individual items of data are the towns and cities and the relationship is one of physical connection through a road system. Such a data type might be used in a system for the scheduling of deliveries by a goods carrier.

SELF TEST QUESTION 9

Which abstract data types would be used to model the following:

▸ The fact that employees in a company are physically located in the same room.

▸ The collection of employees in a company.

▸ The connections between computers in a network.

▸ The relationship between customers and the amount of business that they have given a company over the current financial year.

Figure 2.5 A record

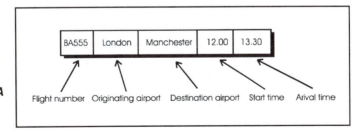

2.3.5 The record

A record is an abstract data type which associates a number of data items. These data items are conceptually linked together. For example, a record used in a personnel system to describe an employee will contain data items which reflect the employee's name, their salary, their national insurance number, any tax information together with other items of data. Each element of such an abstract data type, known as a *field*, is there by virtue of the fact that they are connected; in the example used above they are connected because they are all the properties of the same employee. Figure 2.5 shows an example of a record used in an air-traffic control application.

2.4 Concrete data structures and implementation

A programming language will contain a variety of data structures which provide the basis for an implementation of abstract data types. In Java there is a wide variety of what are known as scalar or basic data types such as `int`, `float`, `long` and `char`. Java also contains facilities for forming arrays and strings and for manipulating pointers; consequently, the implementation of abstract data types is usually a matter of routine.

Later in this book we will look at the topic of implementation in more detail. However, it is worth saying now that there are a number of criteria used to judge an implementation. These are: programming complexity, the storage used and speed. As you will see later in this text there is always some compromise that needs to be made. For example, a fast implementation of an abstract data type will often require more memory than a slower implementation.

As a short example of an implementation consider a set of integers `IntegerSet`. Figure 2.6 shows an implementation which includes the following operations:

▶   `insert`. This inserts an integer into the set. If there is a duplicate integer in the set then a `DuplicateElementException` is created. If the array is full then a `FullSetException` is created.`count`. This returns with a count of the integers in the set.

▶   `contains`. This returns true if a specified integer is in the set and false otherwise.

▶   `IntegerSet`. This is the constructor which creates an array `intSet` to hold the integers. The constructor has a single `int` argument which is the maximum size of the array.

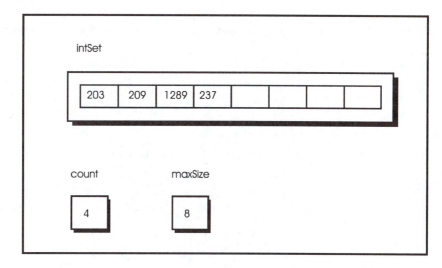

*Figure 2.6 A
simple
implementation
of a set*

The integer array `intSet` contains the integers in the set, while the integer variable `count` contains the number of integers currently stored in the set. The implementation of the insertion operation first checks that the array is not full and then checks that the integer to be added is not already contained in the array. An implementation of `count` returns with the value contained in the `count` variable.

The implementation of the abstract data type contains a private method `contains`. This is used in two of the methods. It works by placing a sentinel at the position `count` in the array and then carries out a linear search of the array. If it encounters the sentinel then the element searched for is not in the array, if it finds the element before encountering the sentinel then the element is in the array.

```
public class IntegerSet{

private int      maxSize;   //Maximum size of the set
private int[]    intSet;    //Array holding the elements of
                            //the set
private int      count;     //Number of current elements in
                            //the set

public IntegerSet(int arg)
{
   count = 0;
   maxSize=arg;
   intSet = new int[arg+1];    //Extra space required for
                               //sentinel
}

public int count()
{
   return count;
```

```
    }

    private boolean contains(int arg)
    {
        //Place sentinel at end of array
        intSet[count] = arg;
        int j=0;
        while(intSet[j]!=arg)
            j++;
        return j<count;
    }

    public boolean in(int arg)
    {
        return contains(arg);
    }

    public void insert(int arg)
            throws FullSetException,DuplicateElementException
    {
        if (count==maxSize)
            //Set is full
            throw new FullSetException();
        if (contains(arg))
            //Duplicate encountered
            throw new DuplicateElementException();
        intSet[count]=arg;
        count++;
    }

}
```

This section has just described one simple implementation, a number of the following chapters will describe implementation issues in much more detail.

CHAPTER SUMMARY

‣ An abstract data type is defined by the effect of its operations.

‣ There are three types of operation associated with an abstract data type: those that return data, those that update the data type and those that update the data type and return some data.

‣ The four main abstract data types are set, map, sequence and graph.

‣ A set contains unique elements.

‣ A sequence is ordered on some criterion.

‣ A map associates items of data with each other.

‣ A graph associates an item of data with another collection of data.

The Implementation of Abstract Data Types

This chapter:

▶ Describes the implementation issues and trade-offs involved in the implementation of abstract data types.
▶ Describes a simple implementation of the set abstract data type.

This chapter looks at the main implementation issues that you will need to bear in mind when constructing large collections of data.

3.1 Introduction

This chapter describes the use of the class facility in Java for developing the code that implements an abstract data type. The data type we have chosen to illustrate the principles involved is that of a set of integers. A number of different implementations are chosen and their differences examined. The operations which are implemented are:

▶ *add*. This adds an integer to the set. I shall assume that the set doesn't initially contain the integer and that the insertion does not exceed the maximum size allowed for the set.

▶ *remove*. This removes an integer from the set. I shall assume that the integer is contained in the set.

▶ *count*. This returns with the number of integers within the set.

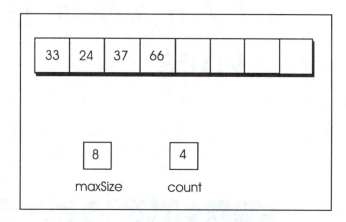

Figure 3.1 A simple implementation of a set

▶ *maxSize*. This returns with the maximum number of items that the set can hold.

3.2 Implementation criteria

There are three criteria that we use to judge implementations. The first is the run-time efficiency of the code—effectively, how fast it runs. The second is the memory usage of the code. The third is the programming complexity. While the first two are relatively easy to understand in terms of criteria the third might puzzle you. It is an important criterion since a lot of the effort in software development is consumed by maintenance: the modification of code once it has been put into service. Maintenance can consume as much as 70% of a company's human resources since, in the lifetime of computer system, there may be many bugs to eradicate and changes in requirements to satisfy. If the code for a system is difficult to read and contains many convoluted chunks of programming it can be a very expensive business keeping it in service.

In general there are trade-offs between these different criteria. For example, well-designed programs that are fast tend to use more memory than programs which are slower. This is a theme that I shall examine in the following sections where a number of different implementations of the set of integers is examined

3.3 The implementations

3.3.1 A simple implementation

The first implementation is a simple one in which the integers in the set are added to an array. The implementation involves an array `holder` which contains the integers, an `int` variable `count` which contains the current number of integers in the set and an `int` variable `maxSize` which contains the size of the set. This is shown in Figure 3.1 for a set which currently contains four integers and has a maximum size of 8 elements. Those of you with a good knowledge of Java might be wondering whether a set could be better implemented using the `Vector` class in Java. This would allow the set to expand. However, the aim of this section is not to teach efficient implementation but to show the trade-offs that are possible. Such implementations will be described later in the book. The code for the instance variables and the methods are shown below:

```java
class SimpleIntSet{

private int    maxSize,     //Maximum size of the set array
               count;       //Count of number of items in set
private int[]  holder;      //Array implementing set

SimpleIntSet(int maxSize)
{
   this.maxSize = maxSize;
   count = 0;
   holder = new int[maxSize+1];   //Extra space for sentinel
}

SimpleIntSet()
{
   this(50);                      //Default of 50
}

public void add(int val)
{
   holder[count] = val;
   count++;
}

public void remove(int val)
{
   int index = findIndex(val);
   //Copy elements after found element
   for(int k = index;k<count-1;k++)
      holder[k]=holder[k+1];
   count--;
}

public int count()
{
   return count;
}

public int maxSize()
{
   return maxSize;
}

public boolean isIn(int val)
{
```

```
    int findIndex = findIndex(val);
    return (findIndex<count);
}

private int findIndex(int val)
{
    //Uses sentinel at position count
    int k =0;
    holder[count] = val;
    while(holder[k]!= val)
        k++;
    return k;
}

}
```

There are two constructors for the class. The first constructs an integer set which has a maximum number of elements based on the parameter `maxSize`. The second constructor uses a default value of 50.

The code for each of the other methods is fairly straightforward. The methods `count` and `maxSize` just return with the corresponding instance variable values. The code for `add` just adds a single integer to the end of the array; the code for `remove` first finds the integer to be removed by a sequential search and then shuffles all the integers after the removed integer by one place upwards; and the method `isIn` just carries out a sequential search for the integer `val` returning the appropriate Boolean value if it is found. The code for the private method `findIndex` uses a device known as a sentinel. The method places the value `val` to be searched for at the end of the array. If this is the item that has been found, then we know that `val` is not in the array; if it is not then it is in the array. Our use of a sentinel means that the constructors have had to allocate one more element than is needed for the array in order to store the sentinel.

It is now worth looking at the criteria that I have set up for judging implementations. First, is it efficient in the use of memory? The answer is yes, apart from losing the sentinel and gaining in programming complexity, it is impossible to think of any way that less storage could be used. Second, is it efficient in terms of speed. The methods `add`, `remove` and `isIn` all process the array element by element. So, the processing that they carry out is proportional to n, the length of the array. As you will see later this is not particularly efficient. What about the complexity of programming? Since the most complex methods in the class only use a sequential search the programming is very simple—the only complication is the programming of the adjustment of integers in the array when one has been deleted by the method `remove`.

GLOSSARY

sentinel – an object placed at the end of an array which simplifies the searching process

SELF TEST QUESTION 1

The code presented above is deficient in that it does not cater for error conditions. Modify it to cater for exception handling which, for example, caters for the insertion of an element which is already contained in the set.

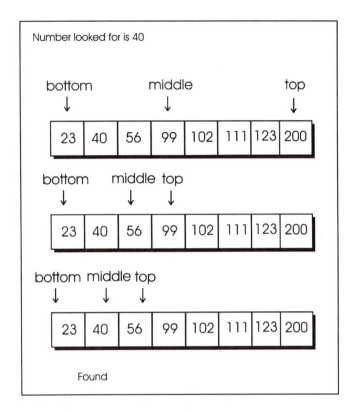

Figure 3.2
The binary
search
mechanism

3.3.2 A sorted implementation

This implementation uses the same instance variables as the previous one. The major difference between that implementation and this one is that the integers in the array are stored in ascending order. Because the integers are in this order we can adopt a more efficient form of processing known as a binary search.

A binary search involves looking at the mid element between two end points for the item to be found. If the element is less than the one at the mid point then the end points are adjusted so the search carries on in the lower half of the array; if the element is greater than the middle one then the search continues in the upper half; and if the middle element is the one searched for, then the search terminates. A typical binary search is shown in Figure 3.2. The code for the class based on this form of storage is shown below:

```
class BinaryIntSet{

private int     maxSize,      //Maximum size of set
                count;        //Number of items in set
private int[]   holder;       //Array used to hold set

BinaryIntSet(int size)
```

```
{
    count =0;
    maxSize = size;
    holder = new int [maxSize];
}

BinaryIntSet()
{
    this(50);                          //Default of 50 in set
}

public void add(int val)
{
    count++;
    //Add the element to the end and keep
    //swapping until the array is back in order
    holder[count-1]=val;
    if(count>1)
    {
        int k =count-1, temp;
        while(holder[k-1]>holder[k])
        {
            temp= holder[k-1];
            holder[k-1] = holder[k];
            holder[k] = temp;
            k--;
            if (k==0)
                break;
        }
    }
}

public void remove(int val)
{
    int indexPosition = findIndex(val);
    for(int j = indexPosition;j<count-1;j++)
        holder[j]=holder[j+1];
    count--;
}

public int count()
{
    return count;
}

public int maxSize()
{
    return maxSize;
}

public boolean isIn(int val)
{
    return findIndex(val)<count;
}

private int findIndex(int val)
```

```
{
   //Set end points
   int top = count-1, bottom = 0,midPoint=0;
   boolean found = false;
   while(!found && top>=bottom)
   {
       midPoint = (top+bottom)/2;
       if (holder[midPoint]==val)
          //Element found
          found = true;
       else
          if (val<holder[midPoint])
             //In bottom half
             top = midPoint -1;
          else
             //In top half
             bottom = midPoint +1;
   }
   if(found)
      return midPoint;
   else
      return count;
}

}
```

The method `findIndex` uses two local `int` variables `top` and `bottom` to delimit the search for the value `val`. It loops repeatedly until either the integer has been found or the search is exhausted with a suitable `boolean` value being returned. The method `add` places the integer to be added at the end of the array and then shuffles it along until the array is ordered again. The method `remove` searches for the integer `val` to be removed using the private helper method `findIndex`. When the integer has been found the items after it are shifted upwards by one.

SELF TEST QUESTION 2

How does this implementation fare with respect to speed, memory and progamming complexity?

3.3.3 A Boolean implementation

The third implementation involves a set where you know the range of the integers which are to be stored. In this case we shall assume that the integers to be stored in the set range from 1 to 100. For this implementation we shall use an array of a hundred `boolean` values. If the integer i is in the set then the $(i-1)$th element of the array will be true and false otherwise (we use the $(i-1)$th element since arrays in Java start at 0). The implementation of this abstract data type is shown below:

```
public class BooleanIntSet{
```

```
private int      count,      //Count of the number of elements
                 maxSize;    //Maximum size of set

private boolean[]  holder; //Array used to implement the set

BooleanIntSet()
{
   count = 0;
   //size is 100 since it will always
   //hold ints between 1..100
   maxSize=100;
   holder = new boolean[maxSize];
   for(int j = 0;j<maxSize;j++)
      holder[j] = false;
}

public void add(int val)
{
   holder[val-1] = true;
   count++;
}

public void remove(int val)
{
   holder[val-1] = false;
   count--;
}

public int count()
{
   return count;
}

public int maxSize()
{
   return maxSize;
}

public boolean isIn(int val)
{
   return holder[val-1];
}


}
```

Here only one zero-argument constructor is used since the maximum size of the array is set by the range of the integers being processed. The rest of the programming is very straightforward. Again it is worth looking at the speed, memory and programming complexity. The speed is optimal as no searching takes place. If we assume that the `boolean` array is implemented as an array of bits then the memory size compares very favourably with the other implementations: it will only be less efficient if the number of values within the set is small. The final criteria (the complexity of the code) is low as all it involves is the reading and updating of individual values within the array `holder`.

SELF TEST QUESTION 3

Write a more general version of the class above which processes sets that range from some lower bound `int` to some upper bound `int`. Also include error processing; for example, checking that when an `int` is added to the set it is within the range specified.

3.4 Comparing the implementations

The last implementation involving an array of Boolean values beats the other two on every count. How has this happened? The reason is that we know more about the data for this implementation than the other implementations. The worst implementation of all was the first which was slow because of its reliance on sequential searching. The second implementation was an improvement in speed since we knew that the data was sorted. The third implementation was even more superior in terms of speed since we knew that the set only contained integers between two limits. In general the more we know about data that is stored: what items are going to be frequently accessed, what items are not going to be frequently accessed, what the limits of the values of the items are, what the statistical distribution of the items are, then the more efficient will be the implementation. Often our knowledge about the data will be application driven; for example, we might know that certain data items are going to be retrieved frequently but, on many occasions, our knowledge is a consequence of the fact that we have structured our data in a certain way. For example, in the second implementation of the set of integers we imposed on the data the condition that it was sorted in ascending order.

3.5 Implementation features

3.5.1 Implementation factors and trade-offs

This chapter illustrates an important idea: there are a number of possible implementations of a data collection. A further idea which is worth exploring here is that each implementation differs in terms of a number of important properties. These are:

▶ *Speed*. Some algorithms are faster than others. For example, the `boolean` implementation is blindingly fast: when an integer is looked up there is very little processing involved, all that is involved is the reading of an array element.

▶ *Programming complexity*. Some implementations of abstract data types take a lot more programming than other implementations. For example, the sorted implementation of the integer set has more complex code than the `boolean` implementation.

▶ *Storage size*. Some implementations of data require much more storage than others. For example, if the Java compiler that processed the `boolean` implementation mapped the boolean array into a collection of bits then it would have much smaller memory requirements than the other implementations.

▶ *Limits of applicability*. Some implementations of data require constraints—often severe—to be adhered to. In our examples above the `boolean` implementation wins out on all the criteria in this section save one: that of applicability.

The four factors above trade-off against each other; for example, a very fast implementation of data will usually require more memory and/or greater programming complexity than a slower implementation. One of the great arts of data design is to select an implementation of a particular data structure which provides an acceptable compromise between each of these factors.

It is important to be able to weigh up and select between these different trade-offs—not only when you are developing your own classes, but also when using existing classes. Later in the book we shall be describing some class libraries which contain many collection classes; an intimate knowledge of factors such as the run-time efficiency of each operation and the memory required for these classes will enable you to select one which is optimal for an application.

3.5.2 Operation factors

As well as trade-offs between different implementations there is often a trade-off between operations. For example, one implementation of a collection of data might result in some of the implemented operations being executed very quickly while others are slow. For example, in the sorted set example the process of retrieving an integer was very fast, while the process of adding an integer to the collection was pretty slow. This is in contrast to the simple implementation where the array was not sorted; in this implementation retrieval was much slower but addition, which involved just placing an integer at the end of the array, was much quicker.

The designer of data must always be aware of the mix and frequency of occurrence of the operations associated with a collection in order to take advantage of this information when selecting an implementation. For example, a designer might be faced with two choices: one which involves a very fast retrieval operation and a slow addition operation vis-à-vis an implementation which has very fast retrieval and very fast addition operations, but a very complex set of algorithms and large storage requirements. If the application required frequent retrieval but the data was very static with few addition operations, then the first implementation would win out.

3.6 General objects

Before leaving this brief chapter it is worth saying something about the generality of the code that will be presented in the remainder of this book. The code that has been presented in this chapter has been specific to the storage of integers. This does not make full use of the power of an object-oriented language. The vast majority of such languages allow the programmer to develop data collections that allow any sort of object to be contained in them. In Java this involves a class known as `Object` which is the superclass of all objects. The next chapter describes the `Object` class in a little more detail.

CHAPTER SUMMARY

▸ There are a number of design trade-offs which must be borne in mind when implementing an abstract data type.

▸ These are ease of programming, memory requirements and speed.

▸ One trade-off often militates against another trade-off.

Implementing Sets

This chapter:

▶ Describes a number of different types of algorithm.
▶ Describes a variety of set implementations.
▶ Shows how a Java collection class can be used in the implementation of a set.

This chapter uses the set as an example to discuss some of the issues involved in implementation, in particular the variety of algorithms and concrete data structures that can be used.

4.1   Introduction

The main task of this section is to describe a number of implementations of sets. It has a number of aims. The first is to provide you with a number of examples of algorithm strategies ranging from simple brute-force to sophisticated random algorithms. The second aim is to demonstrate how to develop general purpose packages in Java. The third aim is to provide you with a tool-kit of set implementations which you can use for your own purposes. Before looking at the implementations it is first necessary to describe two further facilities in Java: the `Vector` class and the `Object` class. The former allows us to save effort in implementing sets, while the latter allows a general-purpose implementation of collections that can store any type of data.

4.2 The `Object` class

Figure 4.1 shows an example of what is known as a class hierarchy.

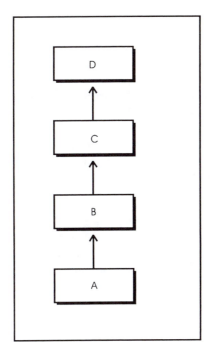

Figure 4.1 A class hierarchy

It shows that class A inherits from class B which then inherits from class C which, in turn, inherits from class D. In object terms we say that A is the subclass of B which is the superclass of A. Within Java all the class hierarchies, both those created by the programmer and those in the Java API class libraries, are rooted in a class known as Object which is provided as part of the Java system. All classes in Java inherit directly or indirectly from Object. Thus classes such as X and Y shown below are assumed to be part of a class hierarchy which is rooted in the Object class.

```
class X extends A{
// Instance variables of X
// Methods of X
}

class Y{
// Instance variables of Y
// Methods of Y
}
```

Even when a class such as Y is ostensibly created without inheriting from another class the Java system assumes that the class will inherit from Object. In the case of class X it will still have Object as one of its superclasses by virtue of the fact that either A does not explicitly inherit from another class (hence implicitly inherits from `Object`) or explicitly inherits from a class which will eventually have `Object` as its superclass.

This discussion of `Object` might seem a little academic; however, it does provide us with the power to develop general-purpose collections of data which can hold objects of any type. However, before looking at how this is done it is necessary to describe a facility within Java known as casting.

There are a number of rules within Java which govern the assignment of objects. The first and simplest rule is that when you have two objects from the same class, identified by say a and b, the assignment statement

```
a = b;
```

is legal and results in a pointing at the object b. The second rule is that if a class A inherits from a class B, either directly or via a number of other classes, and you have an object from A identified by a and an object from B identified by b, then the assignment

```
b = a;
```

is legal. This known as widening. It is illegal to use the assignment

```
a = b;
```

the Java compiler will object. However, a device known as a cast is able to legitimise the assignment. In order to use a cast all you need do is to preface the variable on the right-hand side with the class name of the object on the left-hand side of the assignment enclosed in round brackets. Thus the assignment

```
a = (A)b;
```

is legal. This is known as narrowing. The effect of this is to make visible all the instance variables associated with b which are defined by A.

4.3 The `Vector` class

The previous section described the `Object` class and how casting works. This section describes the collection class `Vector` which is part of the `java.util` library. There are two reasons for describing this class at this stage in the book. First, it is frequently used in the remainder of the chapter and, second, it shows how the `Object` class is used in the development of general-purpose collections. The `Vector` class describes an indexable collection of objects which is extensible; this is in contrast to an array which has a finite amount of space for its contained objects.

There are a number of constructors for the `Vector` class. They specify the initial allocation of elements and the mechanisms whereby the space in a `Vector` is expanded: either by adding a finite amount of space or multiplying the existing space by some factor. For example, the code

```
Vector v = new Vector(100);
```

sets up a `Vector` object `v` with an initial space for 100 elements.

There are a number of methods in the `Vector` class. They carry out standard operations such as adding elements to a `Vector` object, removing elements from a `Vector` object, counting the number of elements and finding out whether an element is contained in a `Vector` object. For example, the method `firstElement()` returns with the first element of a `Vector` and `setElementAt(Object, int)` places the element given by its first argument into the position given by the second argument.

The first argument to `setElementAt` is defined by `Object`. This means that any object defined by any subclass of `Object` (any class) can be inserted into a `Vector`. Thus,

```
AnyClass a = new AnyClass();
Vector v = new Vector(100);
..
..
v.setElementAt(a,12);
..
..
```

is legal, since the implicit assignment to the formal `Object` argument of the `setElementAt` method of the `AnyClass` object is of the form

```
Object variable = AnyClass variable;
```

which is allowable since it represents a widening. Given that a `Vector` object can contain objects defined by `Object` how is it possible to retrieve elements such that they are of the right type? In order to see how consider the code below which uses the `Vector` method `elementAt(int)`. This returns the object that is at the position in a `Vector` given by its `int` argument.

```
Vector v = new Vector(25);
..
..
/*
Code which deposits Aclass objects into the Vector v
/*
..
..
Aclass a = (Aclass) v.elementAt(10);
```

Since `elementAt` returns an `Object` object we need to change the retrieved object to one described by `Aclass` —all that is required is to use a cast.

This is a relatively simple mechanism for storing objects which are described by any class. The implication of using objects described by `Object` are discussed later.

Before leaving this section it is worth describing how scalar data types are stored in collection objects. One of the characteristics of the Java programming language is that it divides data into objects or scalar data types such as `int`s, `char`s or `float`s. Since the latter are not objects they cannot be cast to an object. In order to store such entities in `Object`-based collections Java contains a number of classes known as object wrappers. These classes are found in the `java.lang` package. Each object wrapper corresponds to a scalar data type. For example, the `Integer` class corresponds to the `int` scalar data type.

In order for a variable of a scalar data type to be stored in a collection object which stores objects described by `Object` it has to be converted into the corresponding wrapper class. When they are retrieved they are converted back to scalars. This is shown for `int`s in the code below:

```
Vector v = new Vector(100);
int a;

..
..

/*
Adds the value in a to the Vector v at position 22
*/
v.setElement(new Integer(a), 22);

..
..

/*
Retrieves the value at position 22 in the Vector v
*/
a = ((Integer)v.atElement(22)).intValue();
..
```

The `setElement` method takes an `Integer` object as its first argument. The object is created by using a constructor from the `Integer` class which takes a single `int` argument and creates an `Integer` object which is equal to this argument. The value that has been stored at element 22 of `v` is retrieved by the method `atElement`; this returns an object defined by `Object`. This is then cast to an `Integer` and the `int` value retrieved by using the `intValue` method found in the `Integer` class.

4.4 Implementing sets

In this section we shall examine a number of different implementations of sets. Each implementation will store objects defined by `Object`.

We shall implement the following operations:

▶ *add*. This adds an object to the set.

▶ *remove*. This removes an object from the set.

▶ *count*. This returns with an `int` which represents the number of items in the set.

▶ *isIn*. This returns true if its argument is in the set and returns false otherwise.

4.4.1 A simple implementation

The first implementation is very simple because it is based on using the
Vector class. This is not the most efficient implementation as the Vector
class uses sequential algorithms for methods that carry out actions such as
searching for an object and placing an object at a particular indexed
location. More efficient implementations will be described later

For this implementation we shall use a Vector object as an instance
variable for the class. The code for the class is shown below. It includes
two constructors: the second constructor, which acts as a default, allocates
an initial space for 30 objects, the first constructor allocates an initial
number of objects given by its int argument. The methods throw two
exceptions EmptySetException and NotInSetException. In later
implementations we shall ignore the exceptions, apart from the final
implementation which describes the development of a full-blown class.

```
class SimpleVectorSet{

private Vector v;                //Extensible collection

SimpleVectorSet (int no)
{
   v = new Vector(no);
}

SimpleVectorSet()
{
   this(30);
}

public void add(Object o)
{
   v.addElement(o);
}

public void remove(Object o)
      throws EmptySetException,NotInSetException
{
   if (v.size() == 0)
      throw new EmptySetException();
   if (!isIn(o))
      throw new NotInSetException();
   v.removeElement(o);
}

public int count()
{
   return v.size();
}

public boolean isIn(Object o)
{
   return v.contains(o);
```

```
    }

    }
```

Examine the implementation above and criticise it under the criteria of programming simplicity, memory usage and speed.

A quicker implementation of a set could have been achieved if an array of `Object` objects was chosen, since operations on `Vector` objects tend to be about 10% more inefficient in terms of addition and removal of objects stored in arrays. However, this implementation would also be more complex in programming terms since it would have to cope with the extension of the array when it became full. The implementation above is only of use for small sets (less than, say, eight) where its retrieval performance, based on a linear search within the `Vector` class, is comparable to other implementations.

4.4.2 An ordered implementation

This implementation makes use of the fact that the elements that are stored in the set are ordered. Again we shall implement a binary search similar to the one described in the previous chapter in order to provide a very fast search. The implementation below is of the operations described previously. Again I shall use a `Vector` for the instance variable that holds the data in the collection.

```
class BinaryVectorSet{

private Vector holder;

BinaryVectorSet(int size)
{
    //size gives the initial size of the Vector holder
    holder = new Vector(size);
}

BinaryVectorSet()
{
    //Default constructor initial size of holder is 50
    this(50);
}

public void add(CompObject val)
{
```

```
        holder.insertElementAt(val, holder.size());
        if(holder.size()>1)
        {
            int k = holder.size()-1;
            Object temp;
            //Add the element to the end and keep
            //swapping until the vector is back in order
            while(((CompObject)holder.
                elementAt(k-1)).compareTo(holder.elementAt(k))>0)
                {
                    temp = holder.elementAt(k-1);
                    holder.setElementAt(holder.elementAt(k),k-1);
                    holder.setElementAt(temp, k);
                    k--;
                    if (k==0)
                        break;
                }
        }
}

public void remove(CompObject val)
{
    int indexPosition = findIndex(val),
        count = holder.size();
    for(int j = indexPosition;j<count-1;j++)
        holder.setElementAt(holder.elementAt(j+1),j);
    //set the vector to one less than it was
    holder.setSize(count-1);
}

public int count()
{
    return holder.size();
}

public boolean isIn(CompObject val)
{
    return findIndex(val)<holder.size();
}

private int findIndex(CompObject val)
{
    int top = holder.size()-1,
        bottom = 0,
        midPoint=0;
    boolean found = false;
    while(!found && top>=bottom)
    {
```

```
         midPoint = (top+bottom)/2;
         if (val.compareTo(holder.elementAt(midPoint))==0)
            //Found the object
            found = true;
         else
            if (val.compareTo(holder.elementAt(midPoint))<0)
               //The value is before the mid point
               top = midPoint-1;
            else
               //The value is after the mid point
               bottom = midPoint+1;
      }
      if(found)
         return midPoint;
      else
         return holder.size();
   }

}
```

The most complex method is `findIndex`. This uses two variables `top` and `bottom` to delineate the area of the vector that it is being searched. Each time the search loops the code examines the middle element between these two end points and makes a decision on which half of the area to search further. If the element to be searched for is less than the middle element the top of the search is reset to the middle index of the area to be searched; and if the element to be searched for is greater than the middle element then the bottom of the search is reset to the middle index of the area to be searched. When the middle element is equal to the element that is searched for then the search terminates with a true value returned, if the object is not found then false is returned.

SELF TEST QUESTION 2

Examine the implementation above and compare it with the previous implementation using the criteria of programming simplicity, memory usage and speed.

An important point to make about this code is that the methods operate on objects defined by the class `CompObject`. If we had used objects defined by `Object` then a problem would have occurred: the binary search method requires us to make comparisons using < or >. Unfortunately these operators are not defined for objects of any class. In the code we have had to use a method known as `compareTo`. This has a single `Object` argument and returns an `int` value less than 0 if its destination object is less than the argument, a zero if they are equal and a value greater than zero if the destination object is greater than the argument. This method is used throughout the class.

The use of `compareTo` gives us a further problem in that many of the classes defined in the Java library and all user-constructed classes will not have defined `compareTo`. What is needed is to store objects which have this method defined. The way to do this is via a Java facility known as an interface. An interface contains constants and methods whose code is not defined. An example of the `CompObject` interface is shown below:

```
public interface CompObject{
public int compareTo(Object o1);
}
```

Here only one method is defined (`compareTo`). Any class which implements this method using the keyword `implements` has to supply code for this method. Let us assume that we want to place `String` objects into the `BinaryVectorSet` collection. We will need to define a new class whose objects hold strings and which implements the `compareTo` method. The class is shown below:

```
public class Stringer implements CompObject{

private String st;

Stringer(String st){
    this.st = st;
}

public int compareTo(Object o1) {
    return st.compareTo(((Stringer)o1).st);
}

}
```

The code for `compareTo` within `Stringer` makes use of `compareTo` which is already defined for `String` objects; this returns an `int` in the same way that has been described for `compareTo` with `CompObject` objects.

`BinaryVectorSet` collection objects can now be used. For example, to add some strings to an object `bs` all we need do is:

```
..
BinaryVectorSet sv = new BinaryVectorSet(100);
sv.add("Darrel");
sv.add("William");
sv.add("David");

..
```

This is a fast implementation of a set which uses an algorithm known as a divide and conquer algorithm for searching. It is particularly fast if the method `isIn` is used much more frequently than `remove` and `insert`. It does, however, suffer from one problem which is connected with its generality: every object that it stores must implement the `compareObject` interface. The implication here is that objects described

GLOSSARY

divide and conquer algorithm – an algorithm which successively splits up a problem into smaller sub-problems and then applies itself to these sub-problems by existing classes such as `Integer` and `URL` cannot directly be inserted into our sorted set. You will need to create a new class which implements the interface `CompObject` This is not ideal; however, the implementation that is described in Section 4.4.3 overcomes this problem.

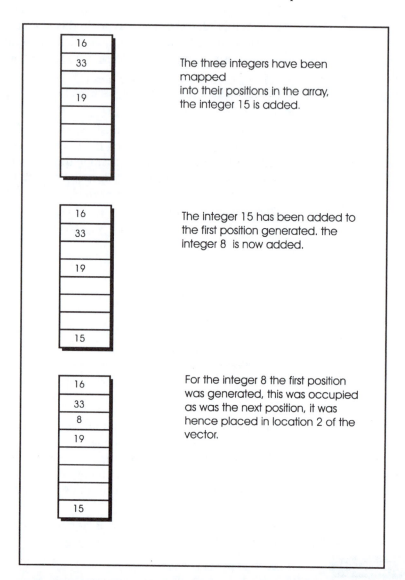

The three integers have been mapped
into their positions in the array, the integer 15 is added.

The integer 15 has been added to the first position generated. the integer 8 is now added.

For the integer 8 the first position was generated, this was occupied as was the next position, it was hence placed in location 2 of the vector.

Figure 4.2 Hashing in action

SELF TEST QUESTION 3

Assume that we wanted to store ordered pairs defined by the class `OrderedPair` in the `BinaryVectorSet`, what would the class definition of `OrderedPair` look like? An ordered pair is a pair of integers with the following rule: that the ordered pair *(a,b)* is greater than the ordered pair *(c,d)* if *a>c;* it is less if *a<c*. However, if *a* is equal to *c* then the first ordered pair is greater if *b>d* and less if *d>b*. They are equal if *a=c* and *b=d*. Since we are dealing with set elements we preclude equality. The code that you write you should implement the interface `CompObject`.

4.4.3 Hashed implementations

This implementation uses something known as a random algorithm. Such an algorithm usually returns a correct result—most of the time very quickly. When it does not return such a result extra work has to be done in order to obtain it. For this implementation we use a rule known as hashing rule which generates a location within a `Vector` or array which determines where an item is to be inserted. Figure 4.2 shows how a hashing rule is used for the insertion of integers into a `Vector`, where a position is generated by dividing the integer by the length of the `Vector` and taking the remainder; in the case of Figure 4.2 the current length of the table is 8.

If you want to check whether an item is contained in the table all you have to do is generate the position using the hashing rule and check whether the item is at that position. This looks very simple and also looks as if it leads to a very efficient implementation: there is no searching involved since the item seems to be located first time.

There is, however, a problem. Some integers will generate the same location when the hashing rule is applied; for example, the integers 9 and 17, and hence there is a need to deal with this. This phenomenon is known as collision and a suitable collision resolution mechanism has to be found. This section describes two such mechanisms. The first mechanism is for the algorithm that carries out the insertion to find the first unoccupied location *after* the location that has been generated and then place the item to be inserted at the location. The algorithm for `isIn` then has two steps: first, generate the initial location; second, if the location contains the object that is needed then return the value true, if not then move down the locations either looking for the object or for an empty location. If the object is found then return true, if an empty location is found then return false. The search for either an empty location or the object to be retrieved will not terminate at the end of the collection when that is reached, but will start again at the beginning of the collection. This is an example of a random algorithm since most of the time we can retrieve the item that is to be searched for quickly; normally if the collection used to store the items is no more than 60% full—and we have a decent hashing algorithm—then no sequential searching is involved and we can get instant retrieval. Since random algorithms cannot be guaranteed to be correct all the time then we have to produce some code for coping with the scarce event of some items mapping to the same locations. One strategy is described in the subsection below.

Linear collision resolution

An implementation of a set which uses hashing is shown below. It uses a
Vector object which is resized when it becomes larger than a factor
defined in its two-argument constructor. The collision resolution strategy
adopted is to fill the next empty location with the object that has caused
the collision. The code for insertion has to start a linear search from the
(occupied) position which it was originally mapped to. The code for the
implementation is shown below:

```java
import java.util.Vector;

class HashSet{

private Vector       holder;         //Vector holding the items
private int          count;       //Count of the number of items
private int          reorgFactor;    //Expressed as percentage

HashSet (int no, int reorgFactor)
{
    holder = new Vector(no);
    this.reorgFactor = reorgFactor;
    count=0;
    //Fill the vector with null values
    for (int j = 0;j<holder.capacity();j++)
      holder.insertElementAt(null,j);
}

HashSet()
{
    //Default of 100 initial locations and reorganisation
    //takes place when the Vector is 60% full
    this(100, 60);
}

public void add(Object o)
{
    int newIndex;
    Vector newVec;
    if(100*count>reorgFactor*holder.capacity())
    {
        //reorganise
        //Double the size
        newVec = new Vector(2*holder.capacity());
        //Initialize the new Vector
        for (int j = 0;j<newVec.capacity();j++)
          newVec.insertElementAt(null,j);
        //Copy over
        for(int k = 0; k<holder.capacity();k++)
        {
            Object n =holder.elementAt(k);
            if(n!=null)
            {
              //If the old location is occupied then copy across
                newIndex =
```

```
                     findIndex(newVec,n,newVec.capacity());
               newVec.setElementAt(n,newIndex);
            }
         }
      holder = newVec;
      }
      //Now add the argument to the resized Vector
      int index = findIndex(holder,o, holder.capacity());
      holder.setElementAt(o,index);
      count++;
}

public void remove(Object o)
{
      //Find the index of the item to be deleted
      int index = findIndex(holder, o, holder.capacity());
      holder.setElementAt(null, index);
      count--;
}

public int count()
{
      return count;
}

public boolean isIn(Object o)
{
      return
         (holder.elementAt(findIndex(holder,
o,holder.capacity())))!=null);
}

private int findIndex(Vector v, Object o, int cap)
{
      //Body of findIndex
}

}
```

SELF TEST QUESTION 4

In the code above the body of `findIndex` is missing. This method takes
three arguments: a `Vector` object, an `Object` object and an `int` which
represents the capacity of the `Vector` object. It returns with the index of
the location that contains the object to be searched for, or the index of the
first location containing the null address if the object is not found. Provide
the code. Assume the existence of a method `hashCode` which returns a
value that can be used to calculate a position for an object. A warning: this
method can return a negative number for some built-in classes such as
`String`.

There are a number of things to note about this class. First, the two-
argument constructor uses an `int` which represents the percentage
proportion of the `Vector` object `holder` which requires reorganisation. So,

45

if this value was 50, reorganisation would take place when the `holder` became more than half full.

The second thing to note is the use of the method `hashCode` used in `findIndex`. This returns a near unique value generated for an object which is to be searched for or be deposited in the set. A number of built-in classes have already defined this method; however, some of them, for example the `String` class, generate a negative number—hence the check for negativity in the code for `findIndex`. If you are using the `HashSet` class with objects defined by your own hand-written classes, then you will need to define a method `hashCode` for them.

The third point to make is about the structure of the `findIndex` method. This takes an `Object` object o, a `Vector` object v and an int `cap` which represents the current capacity of `holder` and generates an index which is the index to the first element of `holder` which is null or matches the argument o. It rotates around `holder` looking for o or the first null location.

The next point to make concerns the method `add`. This reorganises the `Vector` object `holder` when its capacity is such that retrieval would be slow. It sets up a temporary `Vector` object `newVec` which is twice the size of `holder` and then iterates around `holder` extracting out each object and rehashing them into `newVec`.

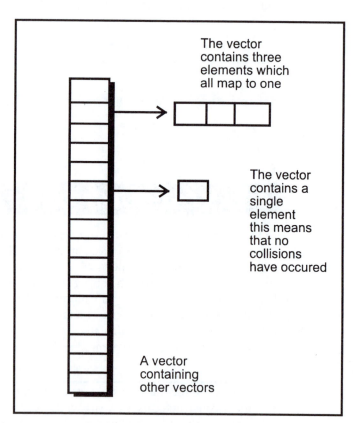

The vector contains three elements which all map to one

The vector contains a single element this means that no collisions have occured

A vector containing other vectors

Figure 4.3 A vector organised for collision containing other vectors

Overflow collision resolution using a `Vector`

Hashed implementations of sets differ in two ways: in their use of different hash calculation methods and in the way they cope with collisions. This implementation uses the same hash calculation method as the previous implementation, but take a radically different view of collision resolution. Instead of looking for the next empty location this implementation will collect all the objects which have the same hash value together. It achieves this by arranging that values are stored in a `Vector` object `holder` whose elements are themselves defined by the `Vector` class, with each element in a `Vector` having the same hash value. This makes for quite a simple implementation and one which is fairly efficient in memory as long as collisions are not too frequent. The implementation is shown in Figure 4.3 for the initial nine locations of a vector. This shows a set containing four elements, three of which map to the same hash value.

SELF TEST QUESTION 5

What can you say about a hash function which carries out the mapping shown in Figure 4.3?

The code for this class is shown below without the code for the methods `remove` and `add`, it does not feature any error handling using exceptions.

```
public class HashVectorSet{

private Vector       holder;      //Holds the items in the set
private int          count;       //Counts the items in the set

HashVectorSet (int size, int overflowSize)
{
    //Create the Vector

    holder = new Vector(size);

    //Add an overflow vector to each vector to hold objects
    //which all map to the same hash value.
    //Normally you can allocate this size as one
    //and the Vector will grow when mapped objects
    //are added to it
    for(int k = 0;k<holder.capacity();k++)
       holder.addElement(new Vector(overflowSize));
    count = 0;
}

HashVectorSet()
{
    this(50,10);
}

public void add(Object o)
{
```

```
        //Code for add
   }

   public void remove(Object o)
   {
      //Code for remove
   }

   public int count()
   {
      return count;
   }

   public boolean isIn(Object o)
   {
      int index = findIndex(o,holder.capacity());
      //Look for the element in the vector
      return((Vector)(holder.elementAt(index))).contains(o);
   }

   private int findIndex(Object o, int cap)
   {
      //Hash value calculated by dividing the hash code
      //by the capacity of the vector and taking the remainder
      //Returns a calculated index, note there is no
      //need for collision handling here
      int hCode = o.hashCode();
      //hashCode can return zero from built
      //in classes such as String!!
      if (hCode<0)
         hCode-=hCode;
      int index = hCode%cap;
      return index;
   }

}
```

An important point to make about the constructor is that it allocates a Vector which contains Vector objects as its individual elements. Each individual Vector contains objects which all map to the same hash value. The constructor allows the programmer to initialise each Vector object inside the main vector to some size; this would normally be 1 for efficiency reasons (we do not want to allocate more space than is necessary). Because a Vector is a growable array, whenever an element is added its size is automatically expanded.

SELF TEST QUESTION 6

Write down the code for the methods add and remove.

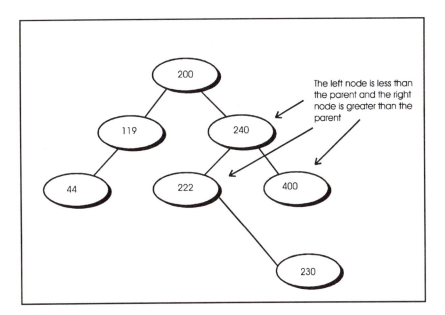

The left node is less than the parent and the right node is greater than the parent

Figure 4.4 A binary tree

The simplicity of this implementation arises from the fact that `Vector` objects are used to hold the collided objects. This means that methods such as `removeElement` and `addElement` can be used, thus replacing complicated coding which would be required if arrays were used to hold the overflowed objects.

4.4.4 A binary tree implementation

This form of implementation uses a dynamic form of storage whereby space is created for objects if and when it is needed. This is in contrast to previous implementations using arrays where for most of the lifetime of the set of objects more space is allocated than is needed.

Here, the items in the set are stored in such a way they contain two pointers to other items. Each item in the set has the property that it points to the left to an item which is smaller and to an item on the right which is larger. For example in Figure 4.4, which represents a binary tree, the integer 200 points to the integer 119 on the left and an integer 240 on the right, with every other item in the tree having this same property. The collection of items is known as a tree and each component of the tree is known as a node. At the top of the tree is a node known as the root; in Figure 4.4 this is the node containing the element 200. In a tree a node which points to another node is known as the parent of the node, the node pointed to is known as the child. In Figure 4.4 the node containing 222 is the parent of the node containing 230 and 230 is the child of the node containing 222.

The implementation of the binary tree requires a subsidiary class `TreeNode` which contains the left-hand pointer, right-hand pointer and data for each of the nodes of the tree. The code for `TreeNode` is shown below:

```
public class TreeNode{

TreeNode    left,        //Left pointer
            right;       //Right pointer
CompObject  data;

TreeNode(TreeNode leftTree, TreeNode rightTree,
        CompObject dataForTree)
{
   left = leftTree;
   right = rightTree;
   data = dataForTree;
}

public TreeNode getLeft()
{
   return left;
}

public TreeNode getRight()
{
   return right;
}

public CompObject getData()
{
   return data;
}

public void setLeft(TreeNode left)
{
   this.left = left;
}

public void setRight(TreeNode right)
{
   this.right = right;
}

public void setData(CompObject data)
{
   this.data = data;
}

}
```

All this class does is to allow access to the various components of a tree node: the left pointer, right pointer and the data (notice the data must be a CompObject since we will be carrying out comparisons on it. The class skeleton for a class `TreeSet` which implements a set as a binary tree is shown below:

```
class TreeSet{

private int count;  //Count of the elements in the tree
private TreeNode pointer;  //Pointer to root

TreeSet()
{
   pointer = null;
   count = 0;
}


TreeSet(CompObject data)
{
   pointer = new TreeNode(null, null, data);
   count =1;
}

public void add(CompObject o)throws InSetException
{
   //Code for add
}

public int count()
{
   return count;
}

public boolean isIn(CompObject o)
{
   //Code for isIn
}


public Enumeration elementsIncreasing()
{
   //Code for elementsIncreasing
}

public Enumeration elementsDecreasing()
{
   //Code for elementsDecreasing
}


public CompObject findMinimum() throws EmptySetException
{
   //Code for findMinimum
}

public CompObject findMaximum()throws EmptySetException
{
   //Code for findMaximum
```

From Data Structures to Patterns

```
    }

    }
```

There are a number of extra methods which have been included in order to provide some material for self test questions. These are findMinimum which finds the minimum element in the set according to the compareTo method; findMaximum which finds the maximum element in the set; elementsIncreasing which gives an Enumeration object that allows us to traverse the elements of the set in increasing order and elementsDecreasing which allows us to traverse the set in decreasing order. The skeleton also includes exception handling code for notifying events such as an object not being found in the set.

The first method to consider is add. The code for this class is shown below:

```
public void add(CompObject o)throws InSetException
{
    if(isIn(o))
        //o is in the tree, throw an exception
        throw new InSetException();
    addIt(o, pointer);
    count++;
}


private void addIt(CompObject o, TreeNode tn)
{
    TreeNode temp = tn;
    if(temp==null)
      //Empty set
      pointer = new TreeNode(null, null, o);
    else
    {
        if(o.compareTo(tn.getData())<0)
        {
            //The item is less than that stored: it
            //is in the left subtree
            temp = tn.getLeft();
            if (temp==null)
                tn.setLeft(new TreeNode(null, null, o));
            else
                addIt(o, temp);
        }
        else
        {
            //The item is greater than that stored: it
            //is in the right subtree
            temp = tn.getRight();
            if (temp==null)
                tn.setRight(new TreeNode(null, null, o));
```

```
        else
            addIt(o, temp);
        }
    }
}
```

This method calls on the helper method `addIt`. What this method does is to check if the current tree is null, in this case a tree consisting of a single node is constructed. If it isn't then it discovers which subtree to add it to based on the content of the tree node that it is examining. Once it has discovered the relevant subtree then it recursively calls itself to add the `CompObject` which is the argument to the subtree. The method `add` throws an `InSetException` if the item to be added is already in the set. Note the use of `compareTo`: the method which needs to be implemented by any `CompObject` which carries out comparisons.

The next method is `isIn`. The code for this is shown below:

```
public boolean isIn(CompObject o)
{
    return isInIt(o, pointer)!=null;
}

private TreeNode isInIt(CompObject o, TreeNode tn)
{
    TreeNode temp = tn;
    if(temp == null)
        return null;
    else
        if(o.compareTo(temp.getData())!=0)
            if(o.compareTo(tn.getData())<0)
            {
                //In the left subtree
                temp=temp.getLeft();
                return isInIt(o, temp);
            }
        else
            {
                //In the right subtree
                temp=temp.getRight();
                return isInIt(o, temp);
            }
    else
        //Found o
        return temp;
}
```

Again this method uses a helper method, this time it is `isInIt`. What this does is to examine the current node that it is processing. If o is held in that node then it returns the address of the node, if it isn't it determines which subtree to look in. For this it takes advantage of the ordering property of the tree: if the object to be looked for lies before the current contents of the node, then the left subtree is examined, otherwise the right subtree is examined. It uses recursion to repeatedly call on itself, splitting the tree into smaller and smaller subtrees until the object is found. If o is not found then the method returns `null`.

SELF TEST QUESTION 7

The method `findMinimum` returns with the minimum object in the set. Write down the code for this method. Throw an exception if the set is empty.

The code for `findMaximum` is similar to that of the answer to the previous self test question; it is shown below:

```
public CompObject findMaximum()throws EmptySetException
{
    if(count()==0)
        throw new EmptySetException();
    TreeNode temp = pointer;
    //Move down every right pointer until null is encountered
    while(temp.getRight()!=null)
        temp=temp.getRight();
    return temp.getData();
}
```

The only difference being that right pointers are processed.

The only two methods which have not been described are those which return `Enumeration` objects: they are `elementsDecreasing` and `elementsIncreasing`; the former delivers the elements of the set in increasing order, while the latter delivers them in decreasing order. Before looking at them it is worth making a slight diversion to revise what the `Enumeration` interface does. Objects derived from this class are associated with a collection: they store information about the collection such as the starting element of the collection, the last element of the collection and how to traverse from one element to another. There are two methods associated with the `Enumeration` interface: `hasMoreElements`, which returns true if the collection has more elements to process and `nextElement` which delivers the next element as an `Object` object.

The built-in collection classes of Java have at least one method which delivers an `Enumeration` object which stores details about the collection. For example, the `Vector` class has a method `elements` which delivers an `Enumeration` object. An example of the use of an `Enumeration` object is shown below. It is used to process a `Vector` object v which contains strings with the contents of the object being displayed on the stream `System.out`.

```
Enumeration e = v.elements();
int count = 0;
while(e.hasMoreElements()){
    String contents = (String) e.nextElement();
    System.out.println
        ("Element "+ count + "of Vector v is "+e); Count++;
}
```

Here the method `elements` delivers an enumeration of the elements of the `Vector` object and the methods `hasMoreElements` and `nextElement` (both belonging to the `Enumeration` interface) are used to iterate over the `Enumeration` object delivered by elements. Since `nextElement` delivers an `Object` object the value delivered, in this case a string, has to be cast.

The code for the method `elementsIncreasing` is shown below:

```
public Enumeration elementsIncreasing()
{
   Vector contents = new Vector();
   collectIncreasing(contents,pointer);
   return contents.elements();
}

private void collectIncreasing(Vector v, TreeNode p)
{
   if(p.getLeft()!=null)
      collectIncreasing(v,p.getLeft());
   v.addElement(p.getData());
   if(p.getRight()!= null)
      collectIncreasing(v,p.getRight());
}
```

The method makes use of the helper method `collectIncreasing`. This recursively collects together all the elements of the tree p by collecting all the elements of the left subtree and the right subtree. It places them in lowest to highest order in a `Vector` object which is the first argument to the method. All the method `elementsIncreasing` then has to do is to return an `Emumeration` of the object.

SELF TEST QUESTION 8

Write down the code for the method `elementsDecreasing`.

4.5 The implementations

In this chapter you have seen a variety of implementations of sets. Each of them exhibited different characteristics.

We started with a simple implementation which used a `Vector` object. This was easy to program, was almost optimal in terms of storage, but suffered from run-time deficiencies by virtue of the fact that it used the linear searching mechanism of `Vector` objects. The second implementation again used a `Vector` object, this time the elements in the `Vector` were ordered. This resulted in an increase in programming complexity but a large increase in speed of search. This implementation was optimal in terms of storage. The third implementation used hashing, it sacrificed storage for a very fast run-time with respect to operations such as adding and searching for an element.

The final implementation was in terms of a tree. This time the programming was quite complex and space was wasted because of nodes in the tree which contained `null` values. However, the run-time of the implementation was fast.

An important point to make about this chapter is that it is the first time that you will have seen the use of high-level data collections such as `Vector` objects in action. Increasingly, as the book proceeds, you will see classes such as `Vector` used more and more in preference to low-level data collections such as arrays. In the chapter that follows a high-level collection known as a `Hashtable` will be used extensively in preference to arrays. This is a consequence of our using an object-oriented programming language; such languages offer rich collection classes which obviate the need for low–level data collections such as arrays.

CHAPTER SUMMARY

▶ There are two ways of implementing sets: using a dynamic implementation or a static implementation.

▶ A static implementation uses a fixed concrete data structure such as an array.

▶ A dynamic implementation uses some pointer-based scheme.

Implementing Maps

CHAPTER OVERVIEW

This chapter:

▶ Describes some implementations of maps.

▶ Shows how the Java `Hashtable` and `Properties` classes can be used to implement a variety of maps.

▶ Shows how collection classes such as `Hashtable` can ease the development of collections.

This chapter continues the theme of showing how basic collections can be developed; however, it also introduces another theme which increases in stress as the book proceeds: that of the use of high-level, built-in classes to develop collections.

5.1 Introduction

An example of a map is shown in Figure 5.1. It shows a map containing data that relates the members in a department to their department.

The left-hand part of the map is known as the domain and the right-hand part is the range. Each element of the map relates an item in the domain to an item in the range. Elements in the range can be simple, or can be complicated objects or collections of objects; for example, the next section describes an implementation where the range is a set of collections.

The important property of a map is that there are no duplicates in the domain, that each element in the domain (known as the key) is not replicated. This means that a map can be regarded as a type of set since the concatenation of each key and its associated element in the range is unique.

There are a number of operations associated with maps. The main ones are:

▸ *add*. This adds a key and its associated value to a map.

▸ *remove*. This removes an item from a map given its key.

▸ *count*. This returns with the number of items within a map.

▸ *isIn*. This returns true if the item (identified by its key) is in the map and false otherwise.

▸ *find*. This returns with the value associated with a particular key.

This chapter will look at variants of these operations applied to two complex maps.

This chapter will look at two classes `Hashtable` and `Properties`. These enable the programmer to easily implement maps within Java. The reason for the comparative shortness of this chapter is that much of the background has been described in Chapter 4 where the hashed implementation of sets was described. This chapter represents a glimpse of a theme which will get stronger and stronger as this book proceeds: the use of high-level collections in preference to low-level facilities such as arrays.

5.2 The `Hashtable` class

5.2.1 Introduction

Java contains the `Hashtable` class which implements maps by means of the hashing mechanism described in Chapter 4. This class has three constructors. `Hashtable (int, float)` sets up a map with an initial allocation of elements given by its first argument and with a load factor given by its second argument; this load factor determines how full the map has to become before more space is allocated to it. For example, a load factor of .5 ensures that the map is reorganised once it becomes more than 50% full. `Hashtable(int)` sets up a map with the number of initial elements given by its argument and with a default load factor. `Hashtable()` sets up a map with a default initial number of elements and a default load factor.

There are a number of methods which can be applied to `Hashtable` objects. Some of the more important ones are described below:

▸ `contains(Object)`. This returns true if the argument is found in the range of the map.

▸ `get(Object)`. This returns with the value associated with the argument. The argument is the key.

▸ `isEmpty()`. This returns true if the map is empty and false otherwise.

▸ `put(Object, Object)`. This adds a key/value pair to the map. The first argument is the key and the second argument is the value.

▶ remove(Object). This removes the object identified by the argument. The argument is the key.

▶ containsKey(Object). Returns true if the key, which is the argument, is found in the Hashtable object.

▶ size(). This returns an integer which is the number of elements in the map.

This class generates maps which can hold objects described by any of the Java base classes. If, however, a programmer needs to store other objects, then he or she has to define a method hashCode which returns an int value based on the contents of the object. This hash value has to have the property that it will have a high probability of being different to hash values generated by different objects of the same class. As an example of this assume that we want to add an object defined by the class ExObj below to a Hashtable.

```
class ExObj{

private int level;
private String name;

// Other methods for ExObj  defined here

public int hashCode()
{
    name.hashCode()+level;
}

}
```

The value that is generated by hashCode is formed by adding the hashCode value of the string instance variable name to the int instance variable level. Note that the class String already has the method hashCode defined for it.

Since Hashtable objects hold objects defined by Object then downcasting has to be used to retrieve values. For example, the code below shows some code in which two items are added to the Hashtable object employees containing employee numbers and names, followed by code which retrieves the name of an employee corresponding to the employee number 34889.

```
//Construction of the Hashtable, .6f is floating point 0.6
//in Java. It ensures that the table will always be
//less than 60% full.

Hashtable employees = new Hashtable(200, .6f);
...
employees.put(new Integer(34889),"J. Davies");
employees.put(new Integer(24891),"W.R.Williams");
...
String name = (String) employees.get(new Integer(34889));
```

GLOSSARY

object wrapper – a class which implements a scalar data type as an object

This code makes use of a concept known as an object wrapper. Since the concept will appear a number of times later in this text it is worth detailing what it does. In an impure object-oriented programming languages such as Java or C++ there are two types of data: objects and scalars. The latter represents basic data types such as integers, floating point numbers—messages cannot be sent to them.

This can be a problem; for example, collection classes such as `Vector` only accept objects; hence, it is impossible to directly store a floating point number or an integer in these collections. It is a problem because we often need to store such entities. In order to get over this, impure languages such as Java provide built-in classes known as object wrappers.

Each of these classes correspond to a scalar data type; for example, in Java there is a class `Integer` which corresponds to the Java `int` data type. There is an easy conversion between the scalar and instances of an object wrapper class: constructors allow the construction of the wrapper object and a number of methods found in the wrapper class convert back to the scalar data type.

5.2.2 An example

This section describes the implementation of a map whose keys are taken from a set of `Object` objects and whose range contains sets of objects with their being implemented using `Vector` objects. An example of such a collection is shown in Figure 5.1 which has a domain that contains the names of departments in a company and a range which contains sets holding the names of the employees who work in the department.

The implementation will use a `Hashtable` object. The skeleton of the class is shown below:

```
public class SetMapper {

private Hashtable holder;

SetMapper()
{
   //Default 200 elements
   this(200);
}

SetMapper(int size)
{
   //Initially has size given by argument and
   //reorganisation factor of.6
   holder = new Hashtable(size,0.6f);
}
```

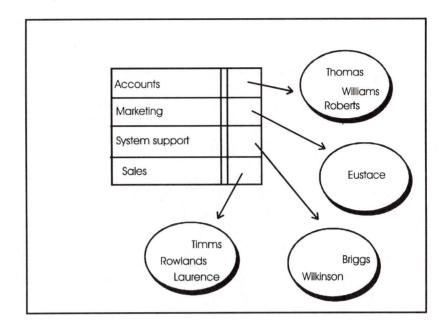

Figure 5.1 A complex map

```
public void addKey(Object key)throws KeyExistsException
{
//Code for addKey
}

public void deleteKey(Object key)throws KeyMissingException
{
//Code for deleteKey
}

public boolean isKeyIn(Object key)
{
//Code for isKeyIn
}

public void addItem(Object key, Object item)
      throws KeyMissingException, ItemExistsException
{
//Code for addItem
}

public void deleteItem(Object key, Object item)
      throws KeyMissingException, ItemMissingException
{
//Code for deleteItem
}

public Enumeration elements()
{
//Code for elements
```

```
}

public Enumeration keys()
{
//Code for keys
}

public Enumeration itemElements(Object key)
      throws KeyMissingException
{
//Code for itemElements
}

public boolean isEmpty()
{
//Code for isEmpty
}

}
```

The implementation uses a `Hashtable` instance variable `holder`. The `Hashtable` maps `Object` objects to `Vector` objects containing a collection of `Object` objects.

The code for the constructors is complete. The one-argument constructor sets up a holder to initially contain `size` locations and it will be reorganised by making it bigger when it is 60% full in order to ensure that its retrieval and insertion performance is fast (0.6f is floating point .6 in Java).

The first method is `addKey`. This adds a key to the map; the key is associated with an empty `Vector` object.

```
public void addKey(Object key)throws KeyExistsException
{
    if(holder.containsKey(key))
      //Key already exists
      throw new KeyExistsException();
    holder.put(key, new Vector(10));
}
```

The method first checks whether the key is already in `holder`, if it is then it throws a `KeyExistsException` exception, if it isn't then it places the key and an empty `Vector` object in `holder`. The second method is `deleteKey`. This deletes the entry in `holder` which corresponds to the argument of the method; both the key and its associated `Vector` object are deleted. For this it uses the `Hashtable` method `remove`.

```
public void deleteKey(Object key)
{
    if(!holder.containsKey(key))
      throw new KeyMissingException();
    holder.remove(key);
}
```

A KeyMissingException exception is thrown if the key cannot be found. The next method is isKeyIn. This returns true if the key can be found in the map and false otherwise.

SELF TEST QUESTION 1

Write down the code for the method isKeyIn. It will need to use the Hashtable method containsKey to do this.

The next method is addItem. This adds the object which is its second argument to the Vector set associated with the object whose key is identifed by its first argument. The code for this is shown below:

```java
public void addItem(Object key, Object item)
        throws KeyMissingException, ItemExistsException
{
    if(!holder.containsKey(key))
        //No key entry found
        throw new KeyMissingException();
    Vector v = (Vector)holder.get(key);
    if(v.contains(item))
        //Item already found in Vector corresponding to key
        throw new ItemExistsException();
    v.addElement(item);
    holder.put(key,v);
}
```

It first checks whether the key is present, if it is then it retrieves the Vector object associated with the key; next it checks whether the object to be added is within the Vector object, if it is then it throws an exception, if it isn't it then it adds the object to the Vector object and updates the key/value pair in holder. If the key is not found then a KeyMissingException exception is thrown.

SELF TEST QUESTION 2

Write down the code for the method deleteItem. This acts in the opposite way to addItem in that it deletes a specific item associated with the key. It should throw a KeyMissingException exception if the key is not found and an ItemMissingException exception if the item to be deleted from the Vector object associated with the key is missing.

The next method is elements, this returns an enumeration of the elements in the map; all it does is to call on the corresponding method within Hashtable.

```java
public Enumeration elements()
{
    return holder.elements();
}
```

The method `keys` provides an enumeration of the keys in the map; like `elements` it just calls on the corresponding method in `Hashtable`.

```
public Enumeration keys()
{
    return holder.keys();
}
```

SELF TEST QUESTION 3

Write down the code for the method `itemElements`. This returns an enumeration of all the items in the map which are associated with a specific key. The method should throw a `KeyMissingException` exception if the key (the method's argument) cannot be found in `holder`.

The final method is `isEmpty`, this returns with a `boolean` true if the map is empty and false otherwise. It just makes use of the `size` method in `Hashtable`.

```
public boolean isEmpty()
{
    return holder.size()==0;
}
```

This concludes the description of this implementation. An important point worth making here is that this implementation of a map containing quite complicated collections has not required very much programming, the reason being that it drew heavily on two of the base collection classes of Java: `Vector` and `Hashtable`. This theme: the reduction of programming complexity through using collection classes will be taken up in Chapter 8 when two modern class libraries for collections will be described.

5.3 The `Properties` class

5.3.1 Introduction

The `Properties` class is similar to the `Hashtable` class and, indeed, inherits many operations from it. However, it differs from `Hashtable` in that it is limited to storing `String/String` pairs and its values are initially stored in a file.

The `Properties` object was originally intended to store system properties in a file which could be easily edited. For example such a file might be used in an operating system to contain a reference to the maximum number of users the system allows and the maximum size of a file to be stored in the system.

A typical `Properties` file is shown below:

```
Motorola=USA
British+Telecom=United+Kingdom
British+Airways=United+Kingdom
Credit+Lyonnaise=France
Telefunken=Germany
```

The string to the left of the = sign is the key and the string to the right is the value. When a space occurs in either the key or the value then an addition symbol is written. The load method transfers the Properties values into the computer memory. This method takes an InputStream as its argument. The save method transfers the data in a Properties object to an output stream. The code below show the use of these methods together with the getProperty method which, given a string key, returns with the value associated with it. The method save has a second argument which is a string. This argument is written to the first line of the Properties object, it is used for identification and is ignored by methods such as put and get.

```
Properties companyDetails = new Properties();
..
/*
Load the Properties object from the file Comp.txt
*/

companyDetails.load(new FileInputStream("Comp.txt"));

/*
operations which modify the Properties object
*/


/*
Look for the company Telefunken in the Properties object and
return the nationality
*/

String nationality =
    companyDetails.getProperty("Telefunken");

/*
Store the updated Properties object in the file Comp.txt
*/

companyDetails.save
   (new FileOutputStream("Comp.txt"),"Company Details");
```

5.3.2 An example

The example which is described here involves a Properties object which stores a key that is the name of an account holder in a bank and a property which is the sequence of account name/balance pairs. The account name is a string and the balance of the account is an int, the pairs are separated by asterisk characters; for example, the line

```
Ince=Account1*234*Account2*245*Deposit*88880*
```

represents the account details of the holder `Ince` who has three accounts `Account1`, `Account2` and `Deposit` with the balance of the `Account1` account being 234 pence.

The skeleton for the class is shown below; the details of each method are described in the text that follows the skeleton.

```java
public class AccountDetails{

private Properties assoc;    //Properties object
private String filename;     //Name of file containing
                             //Properties object

public AccountDetails(String file)
     throws FileNotFoundException,IOException
{
   assoc = new Properties();
   filename = file;
   //Load the Properties object in from file
   assoc.load(new FileInputStream(filename));
}

public int returnNoCustomers()
{
   //Code for returnNoCustomers
}

public void addAccount(String holder, String accountName)
     throws NoAccountHolderException,
          ExistingAccountException
{
   //Code for addAccount
}

private String
    findAccountValue(String acctName, String holderName)
{
   //Helper method
}

public void addAccountHolder(String accHolder)
        throws ExistingAccountHolderException
{
   //Code for addAccountHolder
}

public void terminate()throws IOException
{
assoc.save
   (new FileOutputStream(filename),"Bank account details");
}

public int getBalance(String accHolder, String accountName)
    throws NoAccountException, NoAccountHolderException,
          NumberFormatException
```

```
{
    //Code for getbalance
}

public String [] getAccounts(String holderName)
    throws NoAccountHolderException
{
    //Code for getAccounts
}


}
```

The code for the constructor is already supplied: all it does is to set up the `Properties` data structure by reading it from the file in which it is contained, the file name is an argument to the constructor. The constructor throws two exceptions: the first is thrown if the file was not found, the second if there was a problem in transferring the file to the `Properties` data structure.

The method `returnNoCustomers` returns with the number of customers whose details are held; this just uses the method `size` in the `Properties` class.

```
public int returnNoCustomers(){
    return assoc.size();
}
```

The method `addAccount` adds a specified account to the map; it has two arguments: the first is the name of the holder of the account and the second is the account name. The method throws two exceptions if the holder is not recognised or the account is already associated with the holder. The method uses a helper method `findAccountValue` which employs the Java class `StringTokenizer`. This is a class which has some similarities to the `Enumeration` class. You associate a `StringTokenizer` object with a string and a terminating string via its constructor; the class has a number of methods for traversing the string and extracting out the sub-strings which are ended by the terminating string. The methods used in the code below are `hasMoreTokens` which is true while there are more sub-strings to be processed and `nextToken` which returns the next sub-string in the string. The code for the method and its helper is shown below:

```
public void addAccount(String holder, String accountName)
    throws NoAccountHolderException,ExistingAccountException
{
    //getProperty returns "NotFound" if the key is not found
    String accts = assoc.getProperty(holder,"NotFound");
    if(accts.equals("NotFound"))
        //Key not found
        throw new NoAccountHolderException();
    String accVal = findAccountValue(accountName, holder);
    if (accVal.equals(""))
        {
            //No existing account, set one up with zero balance
```

```
            accts+=accountName+"*"+"000"+"*";
            assoc.put(holder,accts);
        }
    else
        //Account exists throw exception
        throw new ExistingAccountException();
}

private String findAccountValue
        (String acctName, String holderName)
{
    //Helper method
    String acctDetails = assoc.getProperty(holderName);
    boolean found = false;
    StringTokenizer st =
        new StringTokenizer(acctDetails,"*");
    while(st.hasMoreTokens())
    {
        if(st.nextToken().equals(acctName))
            found = true;
            break;
        //Ignore balance
        st.nextToken();
    }
    if (found)
    {
        //Return with the balance of the account
        String val = st.nextToken();
        return val;
    }
    else
        return"";
}
```

The method `addAccount` uses the `getProperty` method of the `Properties` class to check whether the account is already in the map; if it isn't then the method will return the string which is the second argument. If the holder is recognised, the method then uses the helper method `findAccountValue` to discover whether the account is already held by the customer. This method moves down the account/balance pairs using a `StringTokenizer` object until it either reaches the end of the account details or finds the account; if it finds the account it returns the balance of the account, if it does not find the account then it returns an empty string.

The next method is `getBalance`. This takes an account holder and an account name and returns the balance of the account as an `int` value. This method throws three exceptions: the conditions which give rise to these are:

▶ The account holder is not recognised.

▶ The account is not recognised.

▶ The amount returned does not conform to the format of a number; for example, it contains alphabetic characters.

SELF TEST QUESTION 4

Write down the code for the getBalance method. It should use the helper method findAccountValue and the static method parseInt found in the java.lang.Integer class.

The next method is getAccounts which returns with an array of String objects that represent the accounts associated with the holder that is the argument to the method. It uses the StringTokenizer object st to move down the account/balance pairs collecting them up in an array accDetails until the string is terminated.

```
public String [] getAccounts(String holderName)
      throws NoAccountHolderException
{
   String acctDetails =
      assoc.getProperty(holderName,"NotFound");
   StringTokenizer st;
   int count;
   //Assume maximum of 100 accounts
   String[] accsHolder = new String[100];
   if(acctDetails.equals("NotFound"))
      //Account holder is unknown
      throw new NoAccountHolderException();
   st = new StringTokenizer(acctDetails,"*");
   count=0;
   while(st.hasMoreTokens())
   {
      //The loop ignores the account balance in each pair
      accsHolder[count] =st.nextToken();
      st.nextToken();
      count++;
   }
   //Form an array which is the size corresponding
   //to the number of retrieved accounts
   String[] returner = new String[count];
   for(int i=0;i<count;i++)
      returner[i] = accsHolder[i];
   return returner;

}
```

CHAPTER SUMMARY

▶ A map maps elements in its domain to elements in its range.

▶ An element in the range of a map is known as a key.

▶ The Hashtable class is a built-in Java class that implements maps.

69

▶ The `Properties` class is a built-in Java class that implements file-based maps.

▶ Java contains a number of collections that enable abstract data types such as maps to be easily implemented.

Implementing Sequences

CHAPTER OVERVIEW

This chapter:

▸ Revises the notion of a pointer in Java.
▸ Describes a static implementation of a sequence.
▸ Describes a dynamic implementation of a sequence.

This chapter describes the notion of a dynamic implementation of a collection and a static implementation. The latter is an implementation where memory is pre-allocated for the collection: the former is where memory is allocated on demand.

6.1 Introduction

A sequence is a collection of data where the ordering of the data is important. This ordering may be temporal: it may be determined by *when* an item is added to a sequence, or it may depend on some data which might be contained in the elements of the sequence or elsewhere. For example, a sequence of orders in a purchasing system might be ordered on the importance of the companies who are making the orders, with this data stored in a separate part of the purchasing system.

There are two ways of implementing a sequence: using static data structures such as arrays or using a dynamic form of implementation based on pointers. This chapter will examine both. Before doing so it is worth looking at how pointers are implemented in Java since we shall use them extensively in this chapter.

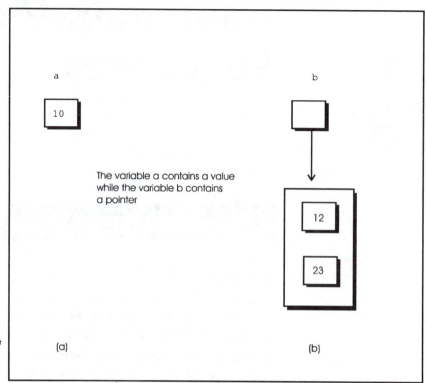

The variable a contains a value
while the variable b contains
a pointer

(a)   (b)

Figure 6.1 The implementation of a scalar data type and an object

6.2 Pointers and Java

Scalar data types such as `int` are implemented by having their identifier label the location where the value is held—this is shown in Figure 6.1(a). However, objects are implemented in a more indirect way. An object is implemented by its identifer labelling a location which contains a pointer to the data associated with the the object. Figure 6.1(b) shows this for an object which contains two `int` instance variables.

This distinction is very important when it comes to assignment. The result of the assignment

```
int x = 22, a = x;
```

and

```
twoInt y = new TwoInt(12,23), b = y;
```

is shown in Figure 6.2(a) and Figure 6.2(b).

The assignment of the scalars (a) creates a new location into which the value of a is placed. The assignment for objects is different: a new location is created, but instead of creating more space for the object all that happens is that the address of the object is copied[1]. You must bear this important fact in mind when reading the remainder of this chapter. You

---

[1] This is the cause of one of the most frequent errors committed by Java programmers. One of the first errors I committed in Java was to write a = b, where a and b were arrays. I was hoping that the contents of b would be copied across to a. Unfortunately all it did was to copy the address of b across.

must also bear in mind that the equality operator == does not compare the contents of objects for equality but compares their addresses.

Thus, in Figure 6.2 the equality (y == b) is true even if you assign a value to b which is different from the old common value shared by y and b. If you want to compare contents, then you need to use the equals method. Many of the objects in the Java API have equals defined for them. However, if you are creating new classes it is worth defining equals for the objects defined by this class, within the class, as a matter of course: almost invariably the users of the class will need such a method.

6.3 Implementing a stack

A stack is a collection in which items which are added last are removed first. There are a number of operations that we will implement:

▶ *push*. This adds an item to the stack.

▶ *pop*. This removes an item from the top of the stack.

▶ *empty*. This returns the value true if the stack contains no elements and false otherwise.

▶ *count*. This returns with the number of items in the stack.

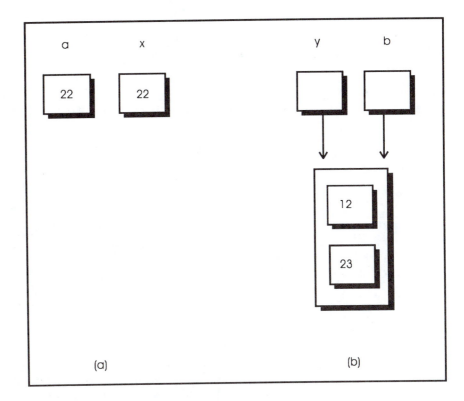

**Figure 6.2
Assignment
for scalars
and objects**

The code uses a `Vector`; this enables us to implement the stack as an extensible collection[2]. The class has an instance variable `holder` which contains the objects in the stack and an instance variable `count` which counts the number of elements in the stack. The method `pop` throws a user-defined `EmptyStackException` if an attempt is made to pop an item from an empty stack. There is one thing of note which we shall not bring to your attention again. This is the use of the `/** .. */` facility which is used by the Java `javadoc` utility to produce HTML documentation for the class. For example, the use of `@return` to describe the object returned by a method. The class skeleton is shown below:

```
/**
Simple dynamic implementation of a stack using a Vector
@author Darrel Ince
@version 1.0
*/

class ExtStack{

private Vector holder;

private int count;

/**
@param The starting size of the stack
*/

ExtStack(int size)
{
    holder = new Vector(size);
    count = 0;
}

/**
@param The object to be added to the stack
*/

public void push(Object o)
{
    //Code for push
}

/**
@return The object at the top of the stack
@exception throws an EmptyStackException if the stack is
empty
*/

public Object pop()throws EmptyStackException
{
    //Code for pop
}
```

---

[2] It is worth pointing out that there is a Stack class in the java.util library. However, it is a slightly impure version of a stack as it extends the Vector class and hence allows access to the middle elements of the stack.

```
/**
@return true if the stack is empty or false otherwise
*/

public boolean empty()
{
   //Code for empty
}

/**
@return The number of items in the stack
*/

public int count()
{
   //Code for count
}

}
```

SELF TEST QUESTION 1

Write down the code for the methods push and pop. You will need to consult the method documentation associated with the Vector class.

The full code for the class including that for count and empty is shown below:

```
/**
Simple dynamic implementation of a stack using a Vector
@author Darrel Ince
@version 1.0
*/

class ExtStack{

private Vector holder;

/**
@param The starting size of the stack
*/

ExtStack(int size)
{
   holder = new Vector(size);
   count = 0;
}

/**
@param The object to be added to the stack
*/

public void push(Object o)
{
   holder.insertElementAt(o, count);
   count++;
```

75

```
    }

    /**
    @return The object at the top of the stack
    @exception throws an EmptyStackException if the stack is
    empty
    */

    public Object pop()throws EmptyStackException
    {
        if(holder.size() == 0)
          //Stack is empty
          throw new EmptyStackException();
        count--;
        return holder.elementAt(count);
    }

    /**
    @return True if the stack is empty or false otherwise
    */

    public boolean empty()
    {
        return (count == 0);
    }

    /**
    @return The number of items in the stack
    */

    public int count()
    {
        return count;
    }

    }
```

6.4 Implementing a simple queue

This section describes two implementations of queues. A queue is a collection where the first item inserted is the first item removed. For the implementations I shall define code for the following operations:

▶ *add*. This adds an item to the end of the queue.

▶ *remove*. This removes the item at the head of the queue.

▶ *count*. This counts the number of elements in the queue.

▶ *inQueue*. This looks for a specified element in the queue and returns true if it is found and false otherwise.

▶ *front*. This returns the first element in the queue.

▶ *elements*. This returns an enumeration of the elements in the queue.

▶ *empty*. This returns true if the queue is empty and false otherwise.

6.4.1 A fixed size implementation

This implementation uses a static data structure such as an array to contain the objects in the queue. The implementation uses two indexes front and back, the former points at the head of the queue, while the latter points at the last element in the queue. As items are added and removed from the queue these indices are incremented. Sometimes the indexes overflow the end of the array and are reset to the beginning of the array. Figure 6.3 shows two states for the queue. Figure 6.3(a) shows the indices following each other with five elements stored and Figure 6.3(b) shows the back index having overflowed to the front of the array with 10 elements stored. This is often called a circular implementation.

The implementation is shown below. The class FixedQueue has four instance variables front, back, count and arraySize. The latter holds the size of the array. There are two constructors: one allocates an amount of space in the array which depends on its argument, the other allocates a default for 100 objects. No error processing is included in the code; for example, it is assumed that an addition to the queue will not overflow the array. The method increment uses the method equals which is defined for all the classes in the Java API. For any other object this needs to be defined in its class definition. The class skeleton is shown below:

```
public class FixedQueue{

private int      count,         //Count of elements in queue
                 arraySize,     //Maximum size of queue
                 front,         //Front of queue
                 back;          //Back of queue
private Object[] holder;        //Holds elements of queue

FixedQueue(int size)
{
    arraySize = size;
    count = 0;
    back= - 1;
    front = 0;
    holder = new Object[arraySize];
}

FixedQueue()
{
    //Default of size 100 elements
    this(100);
}
```

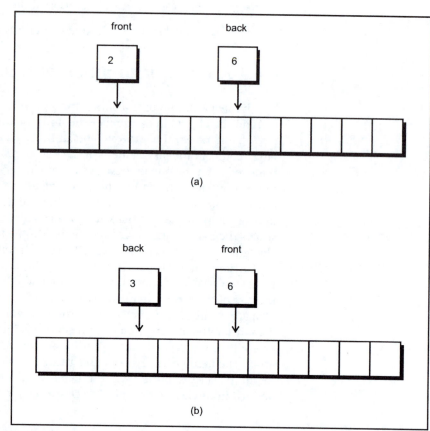

Figure 6.3 A fixed implementation of a queue

```
public void add(Object o)
{
    //Code for add
}

public Object remove()
{
    //Code for remove
}

public int count()
{
    //Code for count
}

public boolean inQueue(Object o)
{
    //Code for inQueue
}

public Object front()
{
    //Code for front
}
```

```
public Enumeration elements()
{
    //Code for elements
}

public boolean empty()
{
    //Code for empty
}

private  int increment(int val)
{
    if(val==arraySize-1)
        val =0;
    else
        val++;
    return val;
}

}
```

The method `increment` handles the housekeeping necessary when incrementing an index to the queue: it moves the index to the beginning of the queue if it overflows the end of the array which contains the queue.

SELF TEST QUESTION 2

Write down the code for the methods `add` and `remove`. Use the helper method `increment`.

SELF TEST QUESTION 3

We need to develop the code for the method `elements`. Before doing this write down the code for an `Enumeration` class which will contain the internal details of the collection.

The `Enumeration` class `FixedQueueEnumerator` described in the answer to the previous self test question has one constructor which allows it to receive details of the important instance variables of the queue. It then provides an implementation of the two methods `hasMoreElements` and `nextElement` found in the interface `Enumeration`. The former returns true if there are more elements in the queue to process and the latter returns the next element in the queue to process. Given this class the code for `elements` is simple:

```
public Enumeration elements(){
return
   new FixedQueueEnumerator(holder, arraySize, front, count);
}
```

All it does is to communicate the array, the array size, front and end of the queue to the `Enumeration` object via its constructor.

The code for the `FixedQueue` class is shown below with the remaining methods having their code filled in. It does not contain any error processing.

```java
public class FixedQueue{

private int     count,          //Count of elements
                arraySize,      //Maximum size of queue
                front,          //Front of queue
                back;           //Back of queue
private Object[] holder;        //Holds elements of queue

FixedQueue(int size)
{
    arraySize = size;
    count = 0;
    back= - 1;
    front = 0;
    holder = new Object[arraySize];
}

FixedQueue()
{
    //Default of size 100 elements
    this(100);
}


public void add(Object o)
{
    back=increment(back);
    holder[back] = o;
    count++;
}

public Object remove()
{
    Object frontValue = holder[front];
    front = increment(front);
    count--;
    return frontValue;
}

public int count()
{
    return count;
}

public boolean inQueue(Object o)
{
    int counter = 0;
    int index =front;
    boolean found = false;
    //Sequential search used
```

```
    while(counter!=count && !found)
    {
        found = holder[index].equals(o);
        index = increment(index);
        counter++;
    }
    return found;
}

public Object front()
{
    return holder[front];
}

public Enumeration elements()
{
    return new FixedQueueEnumerator
                (holder, arraySize, front, count);
}

public boolean empty()
{
    return count == 0;
}

private  int increment(int val)
{
    if(val==arraySize-1)
        val =0;
    else
        val++;
    return val;
}
```

SELF TEST QUESTION 4

What is the main disadvantage of the implementation shown above? How can this be overcome? In answering this question assume that an array is still used.

6.4.2 A dynamic implementation

The previous section described an implementation of a sequence where the size of the sequence was fixed in advance. A better implementation which does not require any wasted space is a dynamic implementation where space is allocated only when it is needed.

For this implementation I shall use a structure known as a linked list. Each element of the linked list will be described by the class `ElementPointer` shown below. All this class contains are instance variables for the data in each element of the list, and a pointer to the next

GLOSSARY

linked list – a collection of data which is linked together via pointers

81

element. The methods are very simple: all they do is to access and set the instance variables of the class.

```
class ElementPointer {

    private Object data;             //The data held in a list
                                     //element
    private ElementPointer next;     //Pointer to the next
                                     //list element

    ElementPointer(Object val)
    {
        data = val;
        next = null;
    }

    public void setData(Object data)
    {
        this.data = data;
    }

    public void setNext(ElementPointer next)
    {
        this.next = next;
    }

    public Object getData()
    {
        return data;
    }

    public ElementPointer getNext()
    {
        return next;
    }

}
```

A linked list is a collection of objects each of which contains an `ElementPointer` object that holds the address of the next object in the queue together with some data. Figure 6.4 shows an example of this form of implementation. Each item in the queue contains the data (not shown) and address of the next element.

The instance variable `head` holds the address of the first element in the queue, the instance variable `tail` holds the end of the queue and the instance variable `count` holds the current number of items in the queue. The last element in the queue contains the `null` pointer.

The skeleton code for the class is shown below. There is only one constructor since a dynamic implementation does not require any information about the maximum size of the sequence. The class skeleton is shown below:

```
class DynamicQueue{

    private int       count;        //Count of the elements
```

```
private ElementPointer  head,   //Head of queue
                        tail;   //Last element in queue

DynamicQueue()
{
   head = tail = null;
   count = 0;
}


public void add(Object o)
{
   //Code for add
}

public Object remove()
{
   //Code for remove
}

public int count()
{
   return count;
}
```

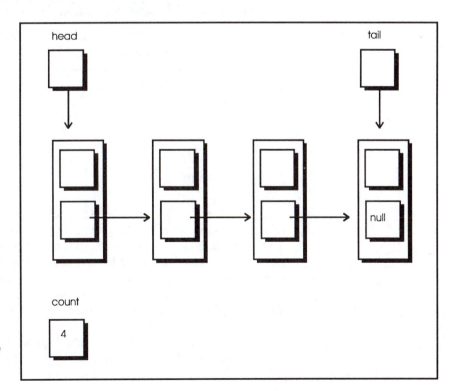

**Figure 6.4 A
linked list
implementation
of a queue**

```
public boolean inQueue(Object o)
{
    //Code for inQueue
}

public Object front()
{
    //Code for front
}

public Enumeration elements()
{
    //Code for elements
}

public boolean empty()
{
    return count == 0;
}

}
```

The constructor just sets the head and tail pointers for the queue to be null and sets the count of items in the queue to zero.

SELF TEST QUESTION 5

Write down the code for the method add. This method will need to add the element o to the end of the list.

The code for remove is shown below:

```
public Object remove()
{
    Object temp = front();
    head = head.getNext();
    count--;
    return temp;
}
```

It removes the object at the front and then resets the variable head to reflect this removal. A question which might have struck you when looking at the code for remove is: what has happened to the object that was removed from the list? What happens is that it is returned to the store of free space that Java maintains[3]. Java implementations all have an automatic garbage collector which periodically examines all the space allocated to objects. Any objects which are not referenced by a variable are returned to the reservoir of free space.

The code for the Enumeration class required for the method elements is shown below. What elements does is to return an Enumeration object

---

[3] This assumes, of course, that the object is not referenced elsewhere.

that allows a programmer to traverse the elements of the linked list. In order to do this there is a need for a class which implements the `Enumeration` interface. This is the class `DynamicQueueIterator` shown below:

```
class DynamicQueueIterator implements Enumeration{

private ElementPointer  traverser;    //Holds the pointer
                                      //that traverses
                                      //the linked list

DynamicQueueIterator(ElementPointer ep)
{
    traverser = ep;
}

public boolean hasMoreElements()
{
    return traverser != null;
}

public Object nextElement()
{
    Object temp = traverser.getData();
    traverser = traverser.getNext();
    return temp;
}

}
```

The code for the two interface methods `hasMoreElements` and `nextElement` is straightforward: the former checks for a null pointer, the latter moves to the next element in the list and returns it.

The code for `elements` is then straightforward:

```
public Enumeration elements()

{
    return new DynamicQueueIterator(head);
}
```

It just returns the `Enumeration` object that refers to the linked list; the programmer can then send the messages `nextElement` and `hasMoreElements` to this object in order to traverse the linked list.

SELF TEST QUESTION 6

Write down the code for the method `inQueue`. It will use an element-by-element search. The answer is provided below.

The full implementation of the queue is shown below:

```
class DynamicQueue{
```

From Data Structures to Patterns

```
            private int                 count;   //Count of the elements
            private ElementPointer       head,    //Head of queue
                                         tail;    //Last element in queue

        DynamicQueue()
        {
            head = tail = null;
            count = 0;
        }


        public void add(Object o)
        {
            if(count==0)
                head = tail = new ElementPointer(o);
            else
            {
                //Adjust last element to point at new element o
                ElementPointer temp = new ElementPointer(o);
                tail.setNext(temp);
                tail = temp;
            }
            count++;
        }

        public Object remove()
        {
            Object temp = front();
            head = head.getNext();
            count--;
            return temp;
        }

        public int count()
        {
            return count;
        }

        public boolean inQueue(Object o)
        {
            ElementPointer traverser = head;
            boolean found = false;
            while(traverser != null)
            {
                if((traverser.getData()).equals(o))
                {
                    found = true; //Element has been found
                    break;            //Exit the loop
                }
            traverser = traverser.getNext();
            }
            return found;
        }

        public Object front()
        {
```

```
        return head.getData();
}

public Enumeration elements()
{
        return new DynamicQueueIterator(head);
}

public boolean empty()
{
        return count == 0;
}

}
```

6.5 Implementing an ordered sequence

An ordered sequence is a sequence where the ordering depends on some data which is either part of the elements in the queue or contained in other objects. These sequences are found frequently in computer systems. For example, an ordered sequence would be used to order the queue of print files which are waiting to be printed in an operating system; with their position based on their priority. In this section we shall concentrate on two implementations, both of which use a list implementation. I shall describe the implementation of the operations described in the previous section with the only difference being that insertion will occur at a point determined by the contents of the element being inserted, rather than the insertion occurring at the end.

6.5.1 A singly linked list

This implementation is structurally the same as the linked list implementation of an ordered sequence described in the previous section. An implementation holding objects of class `Integer` is shown in Figure 6.5. In order to make the processing easy the first element in the queue will contain a value which is larger than all the other values in the sequence. So if priorities between 0 and 999 were to be stored in the queue the first element would contain 1000. This use of a special element, known as a sentinel, simplifies operations such as addition and removal. If we did not use it we would have to program methods which carry out these operations to look for the special case of an empty queue and for the other case: the non-empty queue.

The code skeleton for this implementation is shown below, no error processing is included.

```
class OrderedSequence{

private ElementPointer   header;     //Points at the sentinel
private int              count;      //Count of the elements

OrderedSequence(CompObject o)
```

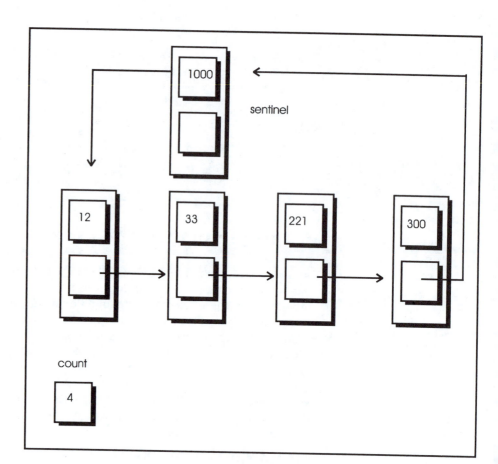

Figure 6.5
A singly
linked list

```
{
    count = 0;
    //Set up the sentinel
    header = new ElementPointer(o);
    header.setNext(header);
}

public void add(CompObject o)
{
    //Code for add
}

public void remove(CompObject o)
{
    //Code for remove
}

public int count()
{
    return count;
}

public boolean isIn(CompObject o)
```

```
{
    //Code for isIn
}

public Object front()
{
    return header.getNext();;
}

public Enumeration elements()
{
    //Code for elements
}

public boolean empty(){
    return count == 0;
}

}
```

The constructor for this class takes a single element that is the sentinel. The methods of this class use CompObject objects as their arguments. Such objects implement the CompObject interface:

```
public interface CompObject
{
public int compareTo(Object o1);
}
```

You will remember that it contains a method compareTo which returns a negative number if its destination object is less than its argument, an integer zero if they are equal and a positive integer if the desination object is greater than the argument.

The reason for using this interface is because we need to compare the contents of the list with the argument of the insertion and removal methods in order to determine where in the list an element is to be inserted or deleted.

The class OrderedSequence uses the class ElementPointer which describes the individual elements in the linked list. This class is defined below:

```
class ElementPointer {

private Object          data;   //The data held in an element
private ElementPointer  next;   //Pointer to the next element

ElementPointer(Object val)
{
    data = val;
    next = null;
}

public void setData(Object data)
{
    this.data = data;
```

```
    }

    public void setNext(ElementPointer next)
    {
        this.next = next;
    }

    public Object getData()
    {
        return data;
    }

    public ElementPointer getNext()
    {
        return next;
    }

}
```

This is a simple class which just contains two instance variables that hold the data in a list element and a pointer to the next list element in the list.
The code for the method add is shown below:

```
public void add(CompObject o)
{
    ElementPointer    traverser = header.getNext(),
                      previous = header;
    //Move over sequence looking for insertion point
    while(o.compareTo(traverser.getData())>0)
    {
        previous = traverser;
        traverser = traverser.getNext();
    }
    //Found it, adjust pointers
    ElementPointer insert = new ElementPointer(o);
    previous.setNext(insert);
    insert.setNext(traverser);
    count++;
}
```

The method loops down the list until it finds the element immediately preceding the insertion point for the object that is to be inserted. When it finds this element it creates a new list element and readjusts the pointers in the list. In order to do this it has to keep track of the previous element in the list to the one being compared, this is held in the variable previous.

SELF TEST QUESTION 7

Write down the code for the method remove. This method will loop down the list looking for the element to be removed and then adjusts the pointers so that it is no longer referenced in the list.

In order for the method elements to be developed we need to construct a class which describes the internal structure of the class and allows access

to individual elements in the sequence. The class needs to implement the
`Enumeration` interface and hence provide the code for the methods
`hasMoreElements` and `nextElement`. The code for this is shown below:

```
class OrderedSequenceIterator implements Enumeration{

private ElementPointer    traverser, //Pointer to move
                                     //around sequence
                          header;    //Head of sequence

OrderedSequenceIterator(ElementPointer header)
{
   traverser = header.getNext();
   this.header = header;
}

public boolean hasMoreElements()
{
   return traverser != header;
}

public Object nextElement()
{
   Object o = traverser.getData();
   traverser = traverser.getNext();
   return o;
}

}
```

The class implements the two methods `hasMoreElements` and
`nextElement` found in `Enumeration`. The former is implemented by
checking that processing has not reached the sentinel; the latter is
implemented by getting the data in the element which is pointed at by the
`traverser` pointer.

The only information required by this class is the head of the list; this is
communicated to it via the constructor. The code for `elements` is then:

```
public Enumeration elements(){
    return new OrderedSequenceIterator(header);
}
```

SELF TEST QUESTION 8

Write down the code for the method `isIn`. This traverses the sequence
until either the sentinel is reached or the element to be looked for is
found.

The full code for the class is shown below:

```
class OrderedSequence{

private ElementPointer  header;      //Points at the sentinel
private int             count;       //Count of the elements
```

```
OrderedSequence(CompObject o)
{
    count = 0;
    //Set up the sentinel
    header = new ElementPointer(o);
    header.setNext(header);
}

public void add(CompObject o)
{
    ElementPointer    traverser = header.getNext(),
                      previous = header;
     //Move over sequence looking for insertion point
     while(o.compareTo(traverser.getData())>0)
     {
         previous = traverser;
         traverser = traverser.getNext();
     }
     //Found it, adjust pointers
     ElementPointer insert = new ElementPointer(o);
     previous.setNext(insert);
     insert.setNext(traverser);
     count++;
}

public void remove(CompObject o)
{
    ElementPointer   traverser = header.getNext(),
                     previous = header;
    //Move over sequence looking for element
    while(((CompObject)traverser.getData()).compareTo(o)!=0)
    {
        previous = traverser;
        traverser = traverser.getNext();
    }
    //Found it, adjust pointers to delete it
    previous.setNext(traverser.getNext());
    count--;
}

public int count()
{
    return count;
}

public boolean isIn(CompObject o)
{
    ElementPointer traverser = header.getNext();
    //Traverse sequence until either sentinel
    //is found or o is encountered
    while((traverser != header) &&
    ((CompObject)traverser.getData()).compareTo(o)!=0)
        traverser = traverser.getNext();
    return traverser != header;
}
```

```
public Object front()
{
    return header.getNext();
}

public Enumeration elements()
{
    return new OrderedSequenceIterator(header);
}

public boolean empty()
{
    return count == 0;
}


}
```

6.5.2 A doubly linked list

Whenever there is a requirement for processing of a sequence to be carried out in both directions a doubly linked list is normally used. In this implementation each element of the list contains a pointer to the next element in the sequence and to the previous element in the sequence. This not only allows a more flexible form of processing but also simplifies some of the programming, although this is at the cost of the extra space involved. An example of such a sequence is shown in Figure 6.6.

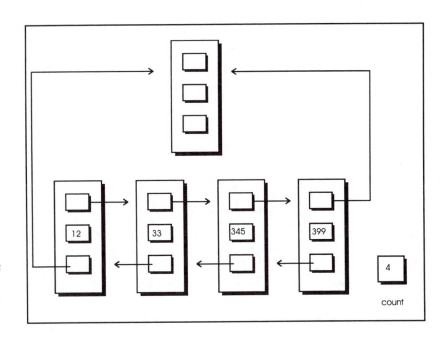

*Figure 6.6
A doubly
linked list*

The implementation presented here will contain no error processing and will make use of the class `ElementTwoPointer` which represents each element of the doubly linked list. This class has three instance variables: one holds the pointer to the previous element in the linked list, another holds a pointer to the next element in the list and the third holds the data held in the element.

```java
public class ElementTwoPointer{

private Object              data;    //Data in an element
private ElementTwoPointer   next,    //Pointer to next element
                            previous;   //Pointer to previous
                                        //element

ElementTwoPointer(Object val)
{
    data = val;
    next = previous = null;
}

public void setData(Object data)
{
    this.data = data;
}

public void setNext(ElementTwoPointer next)
{
    this.next = next;
}

public void setPrevious(ElementTwoPointer previous)
{
    this.previous = previous;
}

public ElementTwoPointer getPrevious()
{
    return previous;
}

public Object getData()
{
    return data;
}

public ElementTwoPointer getNext()
{
    return next;
}

}
```

This simple class just allows access to the instance variables and allows them to be set. The class skeleton for the sequence is shown below, the constructor has one argument which is the sentinel for the sequence.

```
class OrderedSequenceTwoPointer{

private ElementTwoPointer    header;     //Points at the head
                                         //of sequence
private int                  count;      //Count of elements

OrderedSequenceTwoPointer(CompObject o)
{
    count = 0;
    header = new ElementTwoPointer(o);
    header.setNext(header);
    header.setPrevious(header);
}

public void add(CompObject o)
{
    //Code for add
}

public void remove(CompObject o)
{
    //Code for remove
}

public int count()
{
    return count;
}

public boolean isIn(CompObject o)
{
    //Code for isIn
}

public Object front()
{
    return header.getNext();
}

public Enumeration elements()
{
    //Code for elements
}

public boolean empty()
{
    return count == 0;
}

}
```

The code for add is shown below:

```
public void add(CompObject o)
{
    ElementTwoPointer traverser = header.getNext();
    while(((CompObject)traverser.getData()).compareTo(o)<0)
        traverser = traverser.getNext();
    ElementTwoPointer temp = new ElementTwoPointer(o),
                      before = traverser.getPrevious();
    before.setNext(temp);
    temp.setNext(traverser);
    temp.setPrevious(before);
    traverser.setPrevious(temp);
    count++;
}
```

It loops down the linked list until it finds the insertion point; it then creates a list element and adjusts the pointers in the previous and next element to this element so that it is inserted. Note that there is no need for the method to keep track of the previous element in the list via some local variable because this can be found by accessing the previous pointer instance variable in an element.

SELF TEST QUESTION 9

Write down the code for the method remove. This first needs to find the object to be removed; when it is found, the pointers to the previous and next elements to this object are adjusted.

The method elements requires a class which implements the Enumeration interface, this is shown below, only the head of the sequence needs to be communicated to this class; this is done via the constructor.

```
public class OrderedTwoPointerSequenceIterator
            implements Enumeration
{
private ElementTwoPointer   header,     //Points at head
                            traverser;  //Moves around
                                        //sequence

OrderedTwoPointerSequenceIterator(ElementTwoPointer header)
{
    this.header = header;
    traverser = header.getNext();
}

public Object nextElement()
{
    Object temp = traverser.getData();
    traverser = traverser.getNext();
    return temp;
}

public boolean hasMoreElements()
{
```

```
        return traverser != header;
   }

   }
```

The code for `elements` is shown below:

```
public Enumeration elements(){
    return new OrderedTwoPointerSequenceIterator(header);
}
```

The code for the whole class is then

```
class OrderedSequenceTwoPointer{

private ElementTwoPointer    header;    //Points at the head
private int                  count;     //Count of elements

OrderedSequenceTwoPointer(CompObject o)
{
   //Set up sentinel which points at itself
   count = 0;
   header = new ElementTwoPointer(o);
   header.setNext(header);
   header.setPrevious(header);
}

public void add(CompObject o)
{
   ElementTwoPointer traverser = header.getNext();
   //Look for the element insertion point
   while(((CompObject)traverser.getData()).compareTo(o)<0)
      traverser = traverser.getNext();
   //Found it
   ElementTwoPointer temp = new ElementTwoPointer(o),
                     before = traverser.getPrevious();
   //Adjust pointers
   before.setNext(temp);
   temp.setNext(traverser);
   temp.setPrevious(before);
   traverser.setPrevious(temp);
   count++;
}

public void remove(CompObject o)
{
   ElementTwoPointer traverser = header.getNext();
   //Look for element to be removed
   while(((CompObject)traverser.getData()).compareTo(o)!=0)
      traverser = traverser.getNext();
   //Found it
   ElementTwoPointer before = traverser.getPrevious(),
                     after = traverser.getNext();
   //Adjust pointers
   before.setNext(after);
   after.setPrevious(before);
   count--;
}
```

```
public int count()
{
    return count;
}

public boolean isIn(CompObject o)
{
    ElementTwoPointer traverser = header.getNext();
    //Look for element either until it is found
    //or the sentinel is encountered
    while((((CompObject)traverser.getData()).compareTo(o)!=0)
        && traverser != header)
            traverser = traverser.getNext();
    return traverser != header;
}

public Object front()
{
    return header.getNext();
}

public Enumeration elements()
{
    return new OrderedTwoPointerSequenceIterator(header);
}

public boolean empty()
{
    return count == 0;
}

}
```

SELF TEST QUESTION 10

Is the only advantage of this implementation the fact that it reduces the
programming complexity by not requiring the methods add and remove
to continually keep track of the previous element?

In the solution to self test question 10 I described the use of a reverse
iterator. The class code for such an entity is shown below:

```
class ReverseOrderedTwoPointerSequenceIterator
    implements Enumeration{

private ElementTwoPointer    header,      //Points at head
                             traverser;   //Traverses sequence


ReverseOrderedTwoPointerSequenceIterator
    (ElementTwoPointer header)
{
    this.header = header;
    traverser = header.getPrevious();
```

```
}

public Object nextElement()
{
   Object temp = traverser.getData();
   traverser = traverser.getPrevious();
   return temp;
}

public boolean hasMoreElements()
{
   return traverser!=header;
}

}
```

This is very similar to the forward iterator that I defined, the only difference being that the method nextElement moves back to the previous element.

The code for a method reverseElements which delivers this Enumeration object is shown below:

```
public Enumeration reverseElements()

{
   return new
      ReverseOrderedTwoPointerSequenceIterator(header);

}
```

CHAPTER SUMMARY

▶ Three types of sequence were examined: stacks, queues and ordered sequences.

▶ Both dynamic implementations and static implementations were described.

▶ Dynamic implementations tend to lead to complicated code but save on memory.

▶ Static implementations tend to be simpler but are only really suited to small collections of objects.

Combining Classes

CHAPTER OVERVIEW

This chapter:

▸ Demonstrates that collections of data can be built up from smaller collections.
▸ Shows how aggregation can be used to build up collections of data.
▸ Shows how composition can be used to build up collections of data.
▸ Shows how inheritance can be used to build up collections of data.
▸ Provides some examples of aggregation, composition and inheritance in action.
▸ Introduces the UML notation used in the remainder of the book.

This chapter is pivotal in that it represents the boundary between previous chapters which described how simple classes were developed and the remainder of the book which looks at how classes are combined.

7.1 Introduction

All the chapters leading up to this one have described data collections such as sets, sequences and maps whose function can be described quite simply. For example, the actions of adding an element to a set, removing an element from a set and finding the number of items in a set can be described in less than a hundred words. While quite a few computer systems use simple collections, very many combine them. As an example of this consider Web search engines.

The World Wide Web (WWW) represents a massive collection of data, mainly words, which is chaotically ordered. Even in the early days of the

WWW when it was a fraction of the size it is now, users often complained of their inability to find the information that they required. In response to this a number of computer programs known as search engines were developed. These search engines indexed the documents on the WWW and allowed users to pose questions of the index. For example, one of the most popular search engines is Alta Vista, a very powerful program that was managed by the Compaq Corporation. The user of Alta Vista types in a query in very simple query language and Alta Vista will then consult its index to determine which documents satisfy the query. For example, typing in the query

```
relational AND (object OR class)
```

will provide a list of all the Web documents which contain the word *relational* and either the words *object* or *class*. Typing in the query

```
"compiler technology" AND Java
```

will return with a list of documents which contain the phrase *compiler technology* and the word *Java*.

How does Alta Vista and other search engines know about the Web documents and how is it able to associate documents with a key word such as *relational*? One way of organising the collection of data used by a search engine is shown in Figure 7.1[1]. Here two collections are used: a map and a set. The map contains all the keywords of interest to the user and the documents which contain a specified keyword. In this case the key of the map is a string which represents the keyword, while the value is a set of URLs[2] representing each Web document.

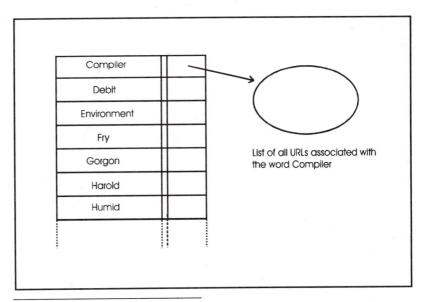

GLOSSARY

search engine – a computer program used to search the World Wide Web

Figure 7.1 Collections of data used by a search engine

---

[1] This is a very simple view of a search engine index, in practice the number of collections and their relationships are much more complex.

101

Aggregation is the process of combining a number of classes together into another class. As an example of this consider the file manager described in Chapter 2. This consists of the following:

▶ A set of blocks of storage that are being used by files administered by an operating system.

▶ A set of blocks of storage that are not being used for files; these are used when the user decides to create a file.

▶ A queue of blocks which are associated with files that have been deleted. Each element of the queue containing a set of blocks which have been released by the deletion of a file.

The classes for this collection of data are shown below

```
class FileHandler{

private BlockSet        usedBlocks,
                        freeBlocks;
private BlockSequence   BlockQueue;

public void addBlockSet(bs:BlockSet)
{
// Code for adding freed blocks to BlockQueue
}

public addFreedBlocks()
{
//Code for adding the head of the queue to freeBlocks
}

//Remainder of methods

}
```

Here the class `FileHandler` contains three instance variables which make up the collection of data that comprises the system for processing file blocks. The `FileHandler` class is composed of these three instance variables.

The relationship that an object contains other types of objects is frequently found in object-oriented systems. There are, in fact, two relationships that you will encounter which describe the fact that objects contain, or are made up, of other objects. They are known as composition and aggregation. They are similar concepts, the only difference lies in the fact that with composition, if an object is deleted all the objects which it contains will be deleted, while with aggregation this does not follow.

Two examples will make this clear. First consider a class which contains the members of a team which carry out some function in a company, perhaps they are a team which has been charged with the task of launching a new brochure. The object representing this team will

---

[2] A URL is a unique string which represents the address of a Web document. It consists of the identity of a computer hosting the document followed by file information which specifies where on the computer the document resides.

contain objects holding the members of the team; the members being employees of the company. When the task is finished the team may be dissolved; however, the objects which make up the team are not deleted: if they are employees of the company then they may join another team. In this case the relationship between a team and the members of the team is one of aggregation.

Second, consider a class that describes employees. An employee object will comprise other objects that describe that employee: objects such as the employee's address and employment history. When that employee is "deleted"—for example, he or she leaves the company—then all the objects associated with the employee are also deleted since they are unique to the employee. I am, of course, assuming here that data is not kept historically on employees that leave. The relationship here is one of composition: when an object is deleted all the objects associated with it are deleted.

You will find aggregation and composition used very frequently. They are used when a class is required which has a state that requires the combination of objects or scalars. A simple example of this form of combination is where an `Employee` class used in a payroll system is built up from the individual components required for salary processing. The skeleton Java code is shown below:

```java
class Employee{

private String    name,
                  address,
                  department,
                  telephoneNo;

private int       salary,
                  taxCode;
//Methods which set and get the values
//of the instance variables
//and carry out functions such as
//calculating the monthly pay

}
```

SELF TEST QUESTION 1

A class is to be used to store details of the collection of users of a computer system, what should be aggregated in this class?

SELF TEST QUESTION 2

The bullet points below describe either a composition or aggregation relationship. Explain which relationship is described.

▶ An operating system consists of a number of sub-systems.

▸ A warehouse consists of a number of products.

▸ A computer consists of a number of specific components.

7.2 Inheritance

There are two main uses of inheritance:

▸ It is used to modify the existing functionality of a class.

▸ It is used to add some functionality to a class.

In both cases a class X is formed by inheriting from a class Y. Class X represents a more specialised (less abstract) version of Y. This will be illustrated by a number of examples.

7.2.1 The augmented set

Consider the set of integers shown below. It is very similar to that presented in Chapter 2.

```
public class IntegerSet
{
private int      maxSize;
private int[]    intSet;
private int      count;

public IntegerSet(int arg)
{
   count = 0;
   maxSize=arg;
   intSet = new int[arg+1]; //End element used for sentinel
}

public int count()
{
   return count;
}

private boolean contains(int arg)
{
   intSet[count] = arg;
   int j=0;
   while(intSet[j]!=arg)
      j++;
   return j<count;
}


public boolean in(int arg)
{
   return contains(arg);
}
```

```
public void insert(int arg) throws FullSetException,
                             DuplicateElementException
{
   if (count==maxSize)
      throw new FullSetException();
   if (contains(arg))
      throw new DuplicateElementException();
   intSet[count]=arg;
   count++;
}

public int findSum()
{
    int temp = 0;
    for(int j = 0;j < count;j++)
      temp+=intSet[j];
    return temp;
}

}
```

The only difference from the set presented in Chapter 2 is that this one contains a method which calculates the sum of the integers held in the set. This represents a simple implementation of a set which is suitable for holding small amounts of integer data. However, let us assume that the findSum method is called a very large number of times and we require a more efficient solution in terms of speed.

One way to achieve this efficiency is to associate an instance variable which holds the sum of the elements in the set; whenever the set is updated by adding another member this variable is updated. This can be achieved via inheritance.

SELF TEST QUESTION 3

What code changes would you make to cater for this new instance variable?

A new class EfficientSet based on the modification described in the self test question above is shown below:

```
class EfficientSet extends IntegerSet{

private int sum;

EfficientSet(int arg)

{
   super(arg);
   sum=0;
}


public void insert(int arg) throws FullSetException,
                             DuplicateElementException
```

```
   {
      super.insert(arg);
      sum+=arg;
   }

   public int findSum()
   {
      return sum;
   }


   }
```

Here the efficiency is achieved by having the `sum` variable updated every time the `insert` method is used. We have traded-off the addition of one simple piece of code at the end of the `insert` method within `EfficientSet` against a `for` loop within `findSum`. Here we have modified the functionality of a class in order to gain an efficiency saving at the cost of the overhead associated with inheritance.

7.2.2 Keeping track of accesses

An example of inheritance used to add functionality is shown below. Here we will use an existing class `Hashtable` from the `java.util` package. As you may remember from Chapter 5, this class provides an implementation of a table which is stored in main memory. Let us assume that we have an application which requires us to know the key and value of the last item added to a `Hashtable` object. This information might be needed in order to take advantage of the fact that after the key and the value have been added they are retrieved very frequently after the addition, without any other key/value pairs being retrieved. If we have the inserted key and value pair stored in instance variables we would just need to consult them without accessing the `Hashtable` object into which they have been inserted. The code for this is shown below:

```
class LastHash extends Hashtable{

private Object  lastKeyAdded = null
                lastValueAdded = null;

public synchronised put(Object key, Object value)
{
   lastKeyAdded = key;
   lastValueAdded = value;
   super.put(key, value);
}

public Object returnLastKeyAdded()
{
   return lastKeyAdded;
}

public Object returnLastValueAdded()
{
   return lastValueAdded;
```

}

}

Here the method `put` within `Hashtable` is overriden with code that updates the instance variables which hold the key and the last object added and then uses the `put` method contained in `Hashtable`.

SELF TEST QUESTION 4

Is this an effective use of inheritance?

SELF TEST QUESTION 5

Can you think of circumstances where the device of using the two instance variables in the code above would be more effective?

At this stage of the book it is worth introducing some notation which describes both inheritance, aggregation and composition. The remainder of the book will deal with increasingly complex collections of objects and a diagrammatic notation will help understanding. The notation I shall use in the remainder of the book is one found in a collection of notations generically known as UML (Universal Modelling Language). The notation that I shall use is known as a *class diagram*. A class is represented by a rectangle with two horizontal lines; above the first horizontal line you will find the name of the class, below the line you will find the instance variables of the class and below the second horizontal line you will find the methods of the class. The notation is flexible in that you can include or not include as much detail as you like; for example, you may decide not to show the instance variables, or to show the instance variables but without their types. Classes which take part in some inheritance, composition or aggregation relationship are linked by special arrows and symbols. They are as follows:

▶ Inheritance is represented by a line with a hollow arrowhead.

▶ Composition is represented by a line which has a filled-in diamond at its end.

▶ Aggregation is represented by a line which has a hollow diamond at its end.

Often, these lines are labelled with some text which describes their function, and numbers at the end of a line which indicate how many instances of an object participate in a relationship. Figure 7.2 shows some of the elements of a class diagram.

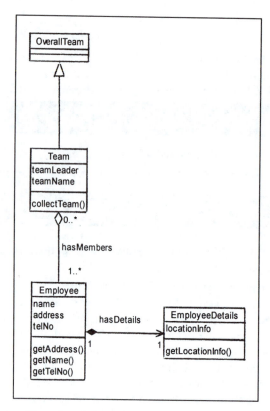

**Figure 7.2
The UML
class
notation**

Here the class `OverallTeam`, whose methods and instance variables are not shown, is the superclass of the class `Team` (the arrow points at the superclass). The class `Team` contains a number of employees defined by `Employee`, with employees having an aggregation relationship with `Team` objects. The relationship is known as `hasMembers`. The numbers associated with this relationship indicate that each `Team` object is associated with 1 or more `Employee` objects and each employee is associated with zero or more `Team` objects (the asterisk in Figure 7.2 stands for *or more*). The `Employee` class shows some of the instance variables and methods associated with the class; for example, `name` is an instance variable, while `getName` is a method. The `Employee` class is associated with a class `EmployeeDetails`. The rectangle for this class only shows a single instance variable and a single method. The relationship is a composition relationship and the numbers indicate that one employee is associated with one `EmployeeDetails` object and only one `EmployeeDetails` object is associated with a single `Employee` object. Each of the relationships is labelled with its name; for example, the fact that a team consists of employees is indicated by the name `hasMembers`.

7.3 Inheritance vs composition

The example at the end of the last section poses an interesting question: which device: composition or inheritance, do you use for developing new collections of data. Inheritance can put quite a high run-time overhead into your programs. Most inherited classes can be rewritten in terms of composition. For example, the EfficientSet class described above can be written as the composition of an IntegerSet and an integer sum as:

```
class EfficientSet{
private IntegerSet    container;
private int           sum;

public IntegerSet(int arg)
{
    container = new IntegerSet(arg); sum = 0;
}

public int count()
{
    return container.count();
}

private boolean contains(int arg)
{
    return container.contains(arg);
}

public boolean in(int arg)
{
    return contains(arg);
}

public void insert(int arg) throws FullSetException,
                            DuplicateElementException
{
    container.insert(arg); sum+=arg;
}

public int findSum()
{
    return sum;
}}
```

Here new versions of each of the methods contained in IntegerSet are developed with the code in each version making use of the methods within IntegerSet.

SELF TEST QUESTION 6

What are the pros and cons of each of the solutions described above?

Object-oriented language compilers are getting more and more efficient and the case for using inheritance over composition where true reuse is required is moving more and more to choosing inheritance. The guiding principle should be that where a class is a specialised version of another class (for example an `EfficientSet` is a special type of `IntegerSet`) then inheritance should be used, in all other cases aggregation or composition should be used.

7.4 A final example

The aim of this example is to describe the processes above in the development of a relatively realistic data collection. The code for the methods are not shown. However, Chapter 9 will describe three large examples of the use of inheritance and composition.

The example is that of a Web browser cache. A Web browser is a program which displays files according to formatting information specified in the text processing language known as HTML. For example, the section of text shown below will be displayed in a Web browser as shown in Figure 7.3.

```
<HTML>
<HEAD>
<TITLE>Example for book</TITLE>
</HEAD>
<BODY>
<H1> Summary </H1>
This summarises the main points of the book
<UL>
    <LI> It is about data.
    <LI> It describes abstract data types.
    <LI> It uses Java as a programming language.
</UL>
</BODY>
```

The document consists of text plus a number of tags which instruct the browser to display the text in certain ways. In the example above the tag pair `<H1>..</H1>` introduces a top-level heading; the tag pair `<UL>..</UL>` introduces a bulleted list and the tag `<LI>` introduces an item of the bulleted list.

One of the problems with Web browsing is that it can take a long time to bring in a file from the Internet and display it using the browser. There are two reasons for this: the Internet can be pretty congested at certain times of the day and the size of the files which are displayed by the browser can be quite large.

Caching is a technique which is used to reduce some of the time that a user has to wait for a Web page to be displayed. It relies on the fact that the user of a browser will often flip between browser files which have been viewed fairly recently. For example, a common occurrence is for a user to browse one file, switch to another file and then return to the original file. A cache is an area of main memory in which the contents of recently browsed files is stored so that if the user of the browser uses one of these files then it is read from main memory into the browser.

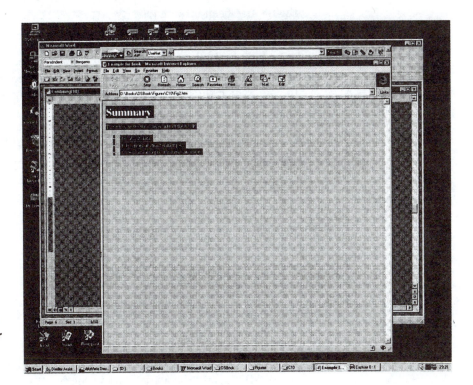

Figure 7.3 A Web browser display

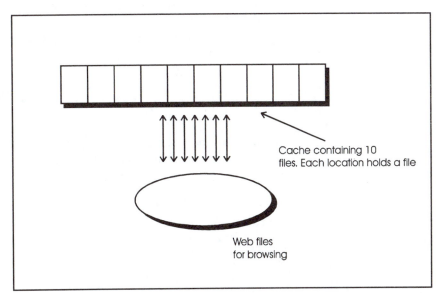

Cache containing 10 files. Each location holds a file

Web files for browsing

Figure 7.4 Cached lists

Figure 7.4 shows an example of some cached files used by a Web browser. Each of the files is stored in an area of memory and is associated with two items of information which can be used by the browser: the first is the time when the file was last browsed, the other is the number of times that the file has been browsed.

It is clear that a cache cannot hold all the pages in the World Wide Web, let alone all the pages that a user has accessed. This means that when a new file, which is not in the cache, is to be browsed which file should be ejected from the cache? The file that should be ejected should be the one which the browser recognises as not being popular with the user. This could be a file which has not been browsed for some time or a file which has not been browsed very much. The former can be identified from the data describing when the file was last browsed, the latter can be identified from the data describing the frequency of access. What classes would be needed for supporting a caching system? First, there would be a basic class describing a file holding a Web Page:

```
class WebFile{

private int        accessFrequency;
private Date       dateLastAccessed;
private HTMLFile   fileContents;
private String     fileName;

//Methods to update and return with the values of
//the instance variables above

}
```

This just uses the composition of the four instance variables used to store the HTML file and the actual data in the file (the details of the class HTMLFile are omitted, just assume that it contains a collection of bytes which represent the contents of a Web browser file).

The next class that is needed is actually a Java interface. The interface shown below contains just one method which delivers the HTMLFile object that needs to be removed in order to bring another HTMLFile object into the cache.

```
interface FileFinder{

private HTMLFile leastPopularFile();

}
```

A class that organises itself by throwing out the file which was accessed very infrequently could then be implemented by inheritance as:

```
class FrequencyCache implements FileFinder{

private [] WebFile   files;
final static         sizeOfCache = 2000;

//Constructors for setting up the cache, the constant
//sizeOfCache holds the number of locations in the array
```

```
//Methods which carry out functions such as placing a file
//in a location in the cache, removing a file from the
//cache. Those methods which remove a file from the cache
//will call upon the method leastPopularFile implemented
//within this class.


private HTMLFile leastPopularFile()
{
//Code which finds the least popular file based on
//frequency of access
}


}
```

The array `files` contains the `WebFile` objects which are to be cached. A class which organises itself by throwing out the which has the earliest time of access could be implemented by inheritance as:

```
class DateCache implements FileFinder{

//Instance variables, cache contains 200 locations

private [] WebFile    files;
final static          sizeOfCache = 2000;

//Constructors for setting up the cache, the constant
//sizeOfCache holds the number of locations in the array


//Methods which carry out functions such as placing a file
//in a location in the cache, removing a file from the
//cache. Those methods which remove a file from the cache
//will call upon the method leastPopularFile implemented
//within this class.


private HTMLFile leastPopularFile()
{
//Code which finds the least popular file based on
//date of access
}


}
```

CHAPTER SUMMARY

▶ Large software systems are constructed from classes which are combined with each other.

▶ There are two mechanisms used for combining classes: aggregation and composition.

▶ Aggregation involves bringing together a number of objects associated with another object.

▶ A special form of aggregation is known as composition where the objects are bound strongly to another object.

CHAPTER 8

Some Modern Class Libraries

CHAPTER OVERVIEW

This chapter:

- Describes the JGL collection library.
- Describes the Java 2 collection library.
- Outlines the relationship between classes in the two libraries and abstract data types described previously in the book.

This chapter is the first introduction to the use of large-scale class libraries which contain collections. Once you have mastered the material in this chapter you should be able to use these libraries with ease.

8.1 Introduction

So far in this book we have looked at the implementation of a number of collections which have different properties. You will have seen how they are built up from basic data types found in the Java language; data types such as arrays. This chapter represents an important change in emphasis as it describes two collection libraries which represent professional implementations of the collections dealt with in previous chapters. The change in emphasis is from developing collection classes to using them.

8.2 JGL

JGL (pronounced juggle) is a class library which was developed by an American company called ObjectSpace[1]. It has been packaged up with a

[1] The library is free and can be downloaded from the Web address http://www.sap.is.ocha.ac.jp/~takefusa/man/jgl3.0.0/index.html

number of development tools including the Integrated Java Development Environment known as Visual J++ which is marketed by Microsoft. All the collection classes available in JGL inherit from a superclass called `Container`. This class defines a number of base methods common to all containers. Some of the more important are:

▶ *add*. This adds an object to a container.

▶ *clear*. This removes all the objects in a container.

▶ *empty*. This returns true if the container contains no elements and false otherwise.

▶ *equals*. This returns true if the objects in a container exactly match those in another container and false otherwise.

▶ *size*. Returns the number of objects in a container.

▶ *maxSize*. This returns with the maximum size of the container in terms of the number of elements it can hold.

▶ *toString*. This converts the contents of a container into a string so that it can be displayed using methods such as `println`.

The code below shows an example that uses the `SList` class provided in JGL. This is a class which inherits from the class `Sequence` which, in turn, inherits from `Container`. `Slist` is an implementation of a sequence using a linked list, where each element is linked via a pointer to the next element in the sequence[2]. This type of implementation was described in Chapter 6.

```
static public void main(String args[])
{
    SList queue = new SList();
    queue.add(new Integer(99));
    queue.add(new Integer(199));
    queue.add(new Integer(202));
    queue.add(new Integer(3));
    System.out.println
        ("Contents of queue = "+queue);
}
```

This creates a new singly linked list and then adds four integers to it. The integers are added sequentially with 99 occupying the first position in the list. The result of this code is to display, on the `out` stream, the string[3] shown below.

---

[2] It might seem strange to advertise the fact that a sequence is implemented in a certain way. On the face of it it might seem to violate the information hiding principle that I described earlier in the book. In fact it doesn't: while the programmer who uses such a class might know what its implementation is he or she cannot write any code which is based on this knowledge. Many class libraries contain alternative implementations of containers such as sequences and it is important to give the programmer some idea of the implementation and their efficiency in order that they can make a choice.

[3] The string concatenation operator + makes an implicit call on the method `toString` defined for `Slist` objects.

```
Contents of queue =SList( 99, 199, 202, 3 )
```

Since the collections in JGL all accept objects defined by `Object` a constructor from the `Integer` object wrapper class is used to create elements which can be added to the `Slist` object. If 'real' objects were to be deposited they can be added directly. For example, the code below adds strings:

```
{
    SList queue = new SList();
    queue.add("Darrel");queue.add("Stephanie");
    queue.add("Alys"); queue.add("Caitlin");
    System.out.println("Contents of queue = "+queue);
}
```

The result of this is the string

```
Contents of queue=SList( Darrel, Stephanie, Alys, Caitlin )
```

being displayed on the `out` stream.

8.2.1 The collections

This subsection describes the collections that are available within JGL; the next subsection describes algorithms which can be applied to containers—such as sorting algorithms. The final subsection describes `Function` objects which are used to apply operations sequentially to containers.

Sets

There are two types of set implemented in JGL. `HashSet` objects store their objects in no particular order. Their implementation relies on the hashing approach described in Chapter 4. The other set implementation is defined by `OrderedSet`. This relies on the search tree approach which is also described in Chapter 4. Here the elements are stored in such a way that the elements are ordered within the collection.

Figure 8.1
The set
classes in
JGL

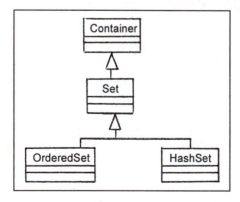

The inheritance hierarchy for sets is shown in Figure 8.1. The set classes are capable of generating sets in which duplicate elements are either allowed or disallowed[4]. Whether a set contains duplicates depends on the constructor used. For example the code

```
HashSet h = new HashSet(true);
```

constructs a set which can contain duplicates, while the code

```
HashSet h = new HashSet();
```

constructs a true set in which duplicates are disallowed.

There are a number of operators for sets. The `union` method forms a set which contains all the elements from two sets; the method `intersection` forms a set which contains the elements which are common to two sets and the method `difference` removes the elements of one set from another set. Thus, the following code

```
static public void main(String args[])
{
    HashSet first = new HashSet(), second = new HashSet();
    first.add("Darrel");
    first.add("Stephanie");
    first.add("Alys");
    first.add("Caitlin");
    second.add("William");
    second.add("Caitlin");
    second.add("Thomas");
    System.out.println("first = "+first);
    System.out.println("second = "+second);
    System.out.println("union = "+first.union(second));
    System.out.println
        ("difference = "+first.difference(second));
    System.out.println
        ("intersection = "+first.intersection(second));
}
```

produces the output:

```
first = HashSet( Stephanie, Darrel, Caitlin, Alys )
second = HashSet( William, Thomas, Caitlin )
union = HashSet( Stephanie, William, Thomas, Darrel,
Caitlin, Alys )
difference = HashSet( Stephanie, Darrel, Alys )
intersection = HashSet( Caitlin )
```

The method `count` will return with a count of the number of objects in a collection which are equal to the argument of the method. If the set disallows duplicates then this value will either be one or zero.

The code

```
static public void main(String args[]){
HashSet first = new HashSet(true); //Allow duplicates
```

---

[4] Strictly speaking this is in contradiction to the normal definition of a set: a collection of objects which has no duplicates. Technically, a set in which duplicates are allowed is a collection known as a bag.

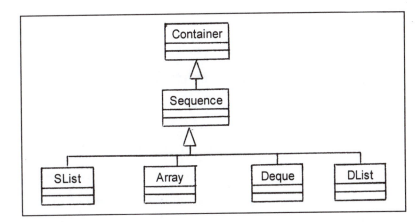

**Figure 8.2
The
sequence
hierarchy
in JGL**

```
first.add("Darrel");
first.add("Stephanie");
first.add("Alys");
first.add("Caitlin");
first.add("Caitlin");
System.out.println
    ("Caitlin occurs "+first.count("Caitlin")+" times");
}
```

will produce the string:

```
Caitlin occurs 2 times
```

Sequences

There are four sequences implemented in JGL. They are:

▶ *Array*. This very similar to the Java built-in class Vector: it is an extensible indexable collection where addition at the end is very efficient.

▶ *Deque*. This is a doubly linked queue which allows fast insertion at its front or end.

▶ *Dlist*. This is a linked list in which each object in the Dlist collection is linked to the previous and next objects via pointers. This is an implementation of the doubly linked list idea described in Chapter 6.

▶ *Slist*. This is a list where each element points to the next element only. This is an implementation of the singly linked list described in Chapter 6.

The inheritance hierarchy for the classes is shown in Figure 8.2.

An example of some of the methods used with a doubly linked queue is shown below. It contains typical methods that you would expect with such a sequence.

```
static public void main(String args[])
{
   DList stList = new DList();
   stList.add("Darrel");
   stList.add("Stephanie");
   stList.add("David");
   stList.add("Robert");
   stList.add("Caitlin");
   System.out.println("List is "+ stList);
   System.out.println("First item is "+ stList.front());
   System.out.println("Last item is "+ stList.back());
   stList.remove(0);
   System.out.println("List is now "+ stList);
   stList.reverse();
   System.out.println("Reverse of list "+ stList);
}
```

The method `front` returns with the first element in the list; the method `back` returns with the final element in the list; the method `remove` has a single argument which is the position of an element within the list which is to be removed from the list; the method `reverse` is a `void` method which reverses the elements in the list. The result of the execution of the above code is:

```
List is DList( Darrel, Stephanie, David, Robert, Caitlin )
First item is Darrel
Last item is Caitlin
List is now DList( Stephanie, David, Robert, Caitlin )
Reverse of list DList( Caitlin, Robert, David, Stephanie )
```

All the sequence classes contain many more methods and HTML documentation on these can be found on the JGL Web site

```
http://www.sap.is.ocha.ac.jp/~takefusa/man/jgl3.0.0/index.html
```

Arrays are very similar to Java `Vector` objects. However, they do have some important properties which distinguish them from vectors. The first is that it is easy to apply the algorithms supplied in the JGL package to `Array` objects; the second is that it is possible to use an `Array` constructor to construct an `Array` object from an existing Java array. As an example of the use of algorithms applied to `Array` objects consider the code below:

```
static public void main(String args[])
{
   Array arr = new Array();
   arr.add(new Integer(88));
   arr.add(new Integer(188));
   arr.add(new Integer(23));
   arr.add(new Integer(2));
   arr.add(new Integer(56));
   System.out.println("Array is "+ arr);
   Sorting.sort(arr);
   System.out.println("Array is now sorted "+ arr);
}
```

*Figure 8.3
Inheritance
hierarchy for
Stack,
PriorityQueue
and Queue*

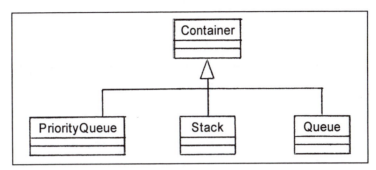

This sets up an array of integers and then uses the static method `sort` to arrange them in ascending order. The result of running the code is

```
Array is Array( 88, 188, 23, 2, 56 )
Array is now sorted Array( 2, 23, 56, 88, 188 )
```

A set of classes in JGL are known as adapters. They are mainly used in connection with Arrays. For example, `ArrayAdapter` objects are arrays which are created from standard Java arrays. This allows the wide variety of algorithms found in the JGL library to be applied to arrays.
Code which takes an `int` array and then sorts the array is shown below; it uses the JGL `IntArray` adapter class which contains `Integer` objects.

```
static public void main(String args[])
{
    int[] intArr = {12, 3, 4, 5, 21};
    IntArray arr = new IntArray(intArr);
    System.out.println("Array is "+ arr);
    Sorting.sort(arr);
    System.out.println("Array is now sorted "+ arr);
}
```

it gives rise to the display shown below:

```
Array is int[]( 12, 3, 4, 5, 21 )
Array is now sorted int[]( 3, 4, 5, 12, 21 )
```

These array classes enable the programmer to treat built-in Java types as container objects and hence apply the rich collection of methods and algorithms in the JGL library to them.

Queues and Stacks

There are three further sequence-like collections in JGL. They are `Stack`, `Queue` and `PriorityQueue`. The inheritance hierarchy which includes these three classes is shown in Figure 8.3. These are all implementations of the collections described in Chapter 6.

The `Stack` class in JGL is very similar to the standard `Stack` class in Java; however, since it inherits from the `Container` class, all the methods defined in this class, together with JGL algorithms, can be applied to objects defined by Stack.

The Queue class supports insertion at its end and removal from its beginning. This is achieved by means of the push and pop methods. An example of these in action is shown below. The code

```
static public void main(String args[])
{
    Queue qHolder = new Queue();
    qHolder.push("Robert");
    qHolder.push("Juanita");
    qHolder.push("Spencer");
    qHolder.push("Don");
    qHolder.push("Anna");
    qHolder.push("Violet");
    System.out.println("Queue is "+ qHolder);
    String taken = (String)qHolder.pop();
    System.out.println("Item removed is  "+ taken);
    System.out.println("Queue is now "+ qHolder);
}
```

generates the display shown below:

```
Queue is Queue( SList( Robert, Juanita, Spencer, Don, Anna,
Violet ) )
Item removed is  Robert
Queue is now Queue( SList( Juanita, Spencer, Don, Anna,
Violet ) )
```

Notice that a cast is used to extract out the first element in the queue since it returns an Object object. Also notice in the display the use of an SList to implement the queue. Probably the most important of the trio of classes is PriorityQueue; this is similar to the ordered sequence described in Chapter 6. This supports all the methods that Queue supports; however, the insertion point of an object within a PriorityQueue is determined by its priority, this is in contrast to a Queue object where an inserted object is placed at the end. The code

```
static public void main(String args[])
{
    PriorityQueue qHolder = new PriorityQueue();
    qHolder.push(new Integer(88));
    qHolder.push(new Integer(2));
    qHolder.push(new Integer(331));
    qHolder.push(new Integer(818));
    qHolder.push(new Integer(13));
    qHolder.push(new Integer(11));
    System.out.println("Queue is "+ qHolder);
    int taken = ((Integer)qHolder.pop()).intValue();
    System.out.println("Item removed is  "+ taken);
    System.out.println("Queue is now "+ qHolder);
}
```

generates

```
Queue is PriorityQueue( Array( 818, 331, 88, 13, 11, 2 ) )
Item removed is  818
```

```
Queue is now PriorityQueue( Array( 331, 88, 13, 11, 2 ) )
```

There are two things of note: first, the display shows that
`PriorityQueue` objects are based on the `Array` class; second, the queue
that we created is stored in descending order. This seems to be the default;
however, what if we wanted to order the queue in other ways; for
example, in ascending order? Happily we can order any `PriorityQueue`
object in any way. It requires us, however, to use a constructor which has
an object defined by the JGL `BinaryPredicate` interface. Later in this
chapter I shall look at predicates and functions in JGL; however, it is
worth taking a peek at the `BinaryPredicate` interface in order to
understand how priorities are implemented.

`BinaryPredicate` is an interface which has one method called
`execute`. This method takes two object arguments and returns true if the
first argument is greater than the second. It is important when you write
the code for `execute` that you do not return true if the object arguments
are equal.

The code for a binary predicate object which compares integers is
shown below:

```
class GreaterInt implements BinaryPredicate{

public boolean execute(Object first, Object second)
{
return
  ((Integer) first).intValue()
      >((Integer) second).intValue();
}

}
```

The code for `execute` takes the two `Object` arguments and converts
them into `Integer` objects and applies the method `intValue` to them to
give an `int` value which can then be compared.

Code in which the constructor uses a `GreaterInt` object is shown
below:

```
static public void main(String args[])
{
    PriorityQueue qHolder =
        new PriorityQueue(new GreaterInt());
    qHolder.push(new Integer(88));
    qHolder.push(new Integer(2));
    qHolder.push(new Integer(331));
    qHolder.push(new Integer(818));
    qHolder.push(new Integer(13));
    qHolder.push(new Integer(11));
    System.out.println("Queue is "+ qHolder);
}
```

This constructs the queue

```
PriorityQueue( Array( 2, 11, 13, 88, 331, 818 ) )
```

It is worth giving another example of a `PriorityQueue` in action. Consider the class shown below which describes files in an operating system:

```
class FileDescriptor{

private int priority;
private String fileName;
private long  fileSize;

public String toString()
{
    return
    "FileDescriptor("+fileName+" "+
    priority+ " " + fileSize +" )";
}

public long  getFileSize()
{
   return fileSize;
}

public int getPriority()
{
    return priority;
}

// More methods follow here

FileDescriptor(String nm, long sz, int pr)
{
    fileName = nm;
    fileSize = sz;
    priority = pr;
}

}
```

It contains instance variables to hold the name of a file, its size in bytes and its priority. The `int` instance variable `priority` determines where it will be placed in a queue for printing. The class also contains a method `toString` which returns with a string version of an object.

The class `GreaterFileDesc`:

```
class GreaterFileDesc implements BinaryPredicate{

public boolean execute(Object first, Object second){
return  ((FileDescriptor) first).getPriority()
        >((FileDescriptor)second).getPriority();
}

}
```

defines an ordering which places `FileDescriptor` objects in ascending order. This means that the code

```
static public void main(String args[])
```

```
{
    PriorityQueue p =
        new PriorityQueue(new GreaterFileDesc());
    p.push(new FileDescriptor("old", 22788, 3));
    p.push(new FileDescriptor("new", 1244, 6));
    p.push(new FileDescriptor("taxes", 2333, 1));
    p.push(new FileDescriptor("table", 223, 8));
    p.push(new FileDescriptor("random", 349, 11));
    p.push(new FileDescriptor("employ", 247, 4));
```

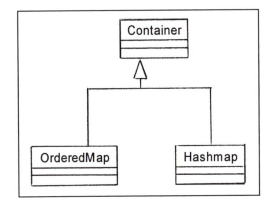

**Figure 8.4
The map
inheritance
hierarchy**

will result in the formation of the `PriorityQueue` object

```
FileDescriptor(taxes 1 2333 ), FileDescriptor(old 3 22788 ),
FileDescriptor(employ 4 247 ), FileDescriptor(new 6 1244 ),
FileDescriptor(table 8 223 ), FileDescriptor(random 11 349 )
```

Maps

Maps in JGL are equivalent to the maps that were described in Chapter 5. There are two map classes `HashMap` and `OrderedMap`. The former is an unordered collection which relates keys to values, the latter is an ordered collection which also relates keys to values. `OrderedMap` objects are used whenever you require an application where there is an association between items and you also want to carry out some sequential processing. The inheritance hierarchy for these classes is shown in Figure 8.4.

There are a number of methods associated with these classes:

▶ Those methods which can be found in the Java `Dictionary` class.

▶ The method `get` which returns with the value associated with a particular key.

▶ The method `add` which, if the key does not exist or if duplicates are allowed, associates the value with the key and then returns the `null` value. Otherwise the table is not modified and the value associated with the key is returned.

▶ The method put which, if the key does not exist in the table, associates the value with the key in the table and returns with null. If the key exists in the table, then the value associated with the key is returned.

Each of the map classes have a constructor that has a Boolean argument; if this argument is true then duplicate keys are allowed to be stored.

The code below shows the use of the put and get methods. The map formed associates byte locations with files defined by the FileDescriptor class outlined in the previous section.

```
static public void main(String args[])
{
HashMap fileTable = new HashMap();
fileTable.put
    (new Integer (8878),new FileDescriptor("old", 22788, 3));
fileTable.put
    (new Integer(99765), new FileDescriptor("new", 1244, 6));
fileTable.put
    (new Integer(9376),new FileDescriptor("taxes", 2333, 1));
System.out.println( "File table is is "+fileTable);
Integer key = new Integer(9376);
System.out.println("\nLocation "+ key+" contains "+
                    (FileDescriptor)fileTable.get(key));
}
```

produces the display:

```
File table is is HashMap
( Pair( 9376, FileDescriptor(taxes 1 2333 ) ),
Pair( 99765, FileDescriptor(new 6 1244 ) ),
Pair( 8878, FileDescriptor(old 3 22788 ) ) )

Location 9376 contains FileDescriptor(taxes 1 2333 )
```

Again, notice that since the keys are int values and put expects an Object, they are converted to objects using the Integer object wrapper. Similarly since get returns an Object object a cast has to be applied in order to change it into a FileDescriptor object.

8.2.2 Algorithms

JGL contains a large number of algorithms which operate on Container objects. There are a number of categories of algorithm:

▶ *Applying algorithms*. These algorithms apply some form of transformation to Container objects. For example, algorithms which add some value to a collection of int values or concatenate a string to a collection of String objects.

▶ *Comparing algorithms*. These algorithms compare two Container objects; for example, to check that they match.

▶ *Counting algorithms*. These count the objects in a `Container` which have a particular property; for example, finding those strings in a `Container` object which have a particular substring.

▶ *Filtering algorithms*. These take a collection of objects and filter out those which do not have a particular property.

▶ *Finding algorithms*. These process a `Container` object and find those objects which satisfy some property. For example, extracting `String` objects which are of a certain length.

▶ *Removing algorithms*. These process a `Container` object and remove objects from the container which satisfy a certain property.

▶ *Replacing algorithms*. These take a `Container` object and replace some or all of the objects in the container according to some programmer-specified criterion.

▶ *Set algorithms*. These correspond to operations such as set intersection and union.

▶ *Rearrangement algorithms*. These rearrange the contents of a `Container` object. These include algorithms for sorting, shuffling and reversing the objects in a `Container` object.

In order to give you a flavour of how these work three examples are presented. Many of these algorithms require JGL `Function` and `Predicate` objects. These will be described in more detail in the next section.

The first example is very simple. It involves the construction of a doubly linked list followed by reversing and then sorting the list.

```
static public void main(String args[])
{
    DList list = new DList();
    list.add(new Integer(99));
    list.add(new Integer(19));
    list.add(new Integer(2));
    list.add(new Integer(1));
    ..
    Reversing.reverse(list); //Note that the method is static
    ..
    Sorting.sort(list);
    ..
}
```

The important point to make about the `sort` and `reverse` methods is that they are static and hence need to be preceded by the name of their class.

The next example involves the element by element processing of a container using an object known as a `BinaryFunction`.

```
static public void main(String args[])
```

```
{
    DList list = new DList();
    list.add("Davis+");
    list.add("Roberts+");
    list.add("Sheen+");
    list.add("DeNiro");
    System.out.println( "List is "+list);
    String result =
            (String)Applying.inject(list,"",new PlusString());
    System.out.println("Result is "+result);
}
```

First a doubly linked list is formed. Next, the static method `Applying.inject` is applied to the list. This method has three arguments: the first is the container which is to be processed, the second is a starting value and the third is an object described by the JGL class `BinaryFunction`. A `BinaryFunction` object has two `Object` arguments to which the function is applied and which returns an `Object` which is the result. `Applying.inject` carries out its third argument by first applying it to its second argument and the object contained in its first argument. In our example, the `BinaryFunction`, we use the built-in JGL function `PlusString` which concatenates two strings. Hence the first thing that the method does is to concatenate the empty string with the first string in `list`. This forms the string `"Davis+"`. Next, it applies the function to this result and the next element in the list, thus forming the string `"Davis+Roberts+"`. It repeatedly does this until the list is exhausted. The result of the program above is thus:

```
List is DList( Davis+, Roberts+, Sheen+, DeNiro )
Result is Davis+Roberts+Sheen+DeNiro
```

The third example shows the use of a JGL `Transforming` method. Some `Transforming` methods take a container and then apply a `UnaryFunction` object to each element in the container. Others apply a `BinaryFunction` object to corresponding elements in two containers and place the result in another container. The example below shows the former.

```
static public void main(String args[])
{
    DList list = new DList(), list1 = new DList();
    list.add("Darrel Thomas");
    list.add("Jane Smith");
    list.add("Joanna Davis");
    list.add("Laurence Thomas");
    System.out.println( "List is "+list);
    Transforming.transform(list,list1,new LengthString());
    System.out.println("New list has become "+list1);
}
```

A doubly linked list is built up. The static method `Transforming.transform` is then applied. This method takes three arguments: the first argument is the `Container` whose objects are to be transformed, the second argument is the container into which the transformed objects are placed and the third argument is the `UnaryFunction` object which is applied to the first argument's objects. In the example above the JGL built-in `UnaryFunction` object `LengthString` is used, this returns with the length of the string to which it is applied.

The result of the execution of the program above is the displayed text

```
DList( Darrel Thomas, Jane Smith, Joanna Davis, Laurence
Thomas )
New list has become DList( 13, 10, 12, 15 )
```

8.2.3 Functions and Predicates

In the previous two sections we have seen the use of functions and predicates in carrying out operations such as transforming the objects in a container. Most of the functions and predicates which I described were built into JGL. The aim of this section is to outline how you can construct your own function and predicate objects.

There are four types of function and predicate objects in JGL: the class `UnaryPredicate` which returns a Boolean value based on a single argument; the class `BinaryPredicate` which returns a Boolean value based on two arguments; the class `UnaryFunction` which returns an `Object` based on a single argument, and the class `BinaryFunction` which returns an `Object` based on two arguments. The arguments to predicates and functions take objects and the result of function application are objects described by the class `Object`, so casting has to be extensively used.

To construct a predicate or function you need to implement a JGL interface. The four that you use are `UnaryFunction`, `BinaryFunction`, `UnaryPredicate` and `BinaryPredicate`. In order to create a `UnaryFunction` you need to implement a method called `execute` which takes a single `Object` argument and returns an `Object`. To create a `BinaryFunction` you need to implement `execute` with two arguments and return an `Object`. To create a `UnaryPredicate` you need to implement `execute` with an `Object` argument and return a `boolean` value, and to create a `BinaryPredicate` you need to implement `execute` with two `Object` arguments and return a `boolean` value.

Four examples are described below. The first describes a `UnaryPredicate` object which returns true if the first character of its `String` argument is a digit.

```
class Leading implements UnaryPredicate{

public boolean execute(Object object)
{
    return Character.isDigit(((String) object).charAt(0));
```

```
}

}
```

The second example describes a binary predicate which returns true if its first `String` argument contains the same leading character as its second `String` argument.

```
class SameChar implements BinaryPredicate{

public boolean execute(Object object1, Object object2)
{
   return
     ((String)object1).charAt(0)==((String)object2).charAt(0);
}

}
```

The third example is the implementation of a `UnaryFunction` which returns the number of digits in its string argument.

```
class CountDigits implements UnaryFunction{

public Object execute(Object object)
{
    String val = (String) object;
    int sum = 0;
    for(int j = 0;j<val.length();j++)
       if (Character.isDigit(val.charAt(j)))
          sum++;
    return (new Integer(sum));
}

}
```

The fourth example is the implementation of a `BinaryFunction` which returns with the count of the digits in both its `String` arguments.

```
class CountTwoDigits implements BinaryFunction{

public Object execute(Object object1, Object object2)
{
    String val1 = (String) object1,
           val2 = (String) object2;
    int   sum1 = 0,
          sum2 = 0;
    for(int j = 0;j<val1.length();j++)
      if (Character.isDigit(val1.charAt(j)))
         sum1++;
    for(int j = 0;j<val2.length();j++)
       if (Character.isDigit(val2.charAt(j)))
          sum2++;
    return
       (new Integer(sum1+sum2));
}

}
```

Category	Class
Sets	HashSet
	TreeSet
Lists(sequences)	Vector
	Stack
	LinkedList
	ArrayList
Maps	Hashtable
	HashMap
	WeakHashMap
	TreeMap

Table 8.1
The Java 2
collection
classes

8.3 The Java 2 collection library

8.3.1 Introduction

The most recent release of Java increased the number of collections available to the programmer to ten. One of the criticisms of the previous releases of the language was the small number of collections that were available. Previously, programmers were only able to use the Vector, Stack and Hashtable classes; now they can use a variety of classes similar in scope to the JGL classes. Table 8.1 shows these classes.

Each of the collections are described below:

▶ HashSet. This is a set implementation which uses hashing; storage and retrieval tend to be very fast with this collection.

▶ TreeSet. This is an implementation of a set which orders the elements in the set. This means that the set elements can be retrieved in some order.

▶ Vector. An implementation of an extensible array. This has not changed since the first release of Java.

▶ Stack. A last-in first-out collection. This has not changed since the last release of Java.

▶ LinkedList. An implementation of a sequence where a pointer from each element in the sequence leads to the next element.

▶ ArrayList. An implementation of an extensible array which can be accessed as a linked list.

▶ Hashtable. An implementation of a map which has been around since the first implementation of Java.

▶ HashMap. A map that is able to store null objects and is able to cope with null keys.

▶ WeakHashMap. An implementation of a map such that when the key to an object is no longer referenced then the key/value pair disappears in that it is garbage collected.

▶ TreeMap. A map where the objects are arranged in ascending order.

Table 8.2 interfaces and collections

Interface	Collections which implement them
Set	HashSet, TreeSet
List	Vector, Stack, ArrayList,LinkedList
Map	Hashtable, TreeMap, HashMap, WeakHashMap

All the classes above can be found in the java.util package. In this package there are three basic interfaces Set, List and Map which are the superclasses of all the collection classes within java.util. Each of these contain common operations, such as add, which can be applied to the collections which implement them. The interfaces, and the classes which implement them, are shown in Table 8.2.

The next two sections describe some of the methods associated with these classes, concentrating on the Set and List collections.

8.3.2 The Set interface

This class is the analogue of the Set class found in the JGL library. A selection of its methods are shown below:

▶ size. This returns the number of elements in the set.

▶ contains. This returns true if its argument is contained in the set and false otherwise.

▶ add. This adds an element to a set.

▶ remove. This removes an element from a set.

▶ clear. This removes all the elements from a set.

A fragment of code involving a Java 2 set is shown below. It first adds five strings to a set, removes one and then displays the size of the set.

```
public static void main(String[] args)
{
    HashSet hs = new HashSet();
    hs.add("Darrel");
    hs.add("William");
    hs.add("Arthur");
    hs.add("Timothy");
    hs.add("David");
```

```
        System.out.println("Set is "+hs);
        hs.remove("David");
        System.out.println("Set is now "+hs);
        System.out.println("The size of the set is "+hs.size());
}
```

This produces the display

```
Set is [Timothy, Darrel, Arthur, William, David]
Set is now [Timothy, Darrel, Arthur, William]
The size of the set is 4
```

8.3.3 The `List` interface

A similar fragment to the one above is shown below; this time it involves a
sequence implemented as a linked list object. It inserts six `Integer` objects
into the list, followed by the removal of one of the objects. It then displays
the first and last elements in the list using the methods `getFirst` and
`getLast`.

```
public static void main(String[] args)
{
    LinkedList ls = new LinkedList();
    ls.add(new Integer(22));
    ls.add(new Integer(300));
    ls.add(new Integer(99));
    ls.add(new Integer(100));
    ls.add(new Integer(2));
    ls.add(new Integer(3));
    System.out.println("List is "+ls);
    ls.remove(new Integer(2));
    System.out.println("List is now "+ls);
    System.out.println("The size of the list is "+ls.size());
    System.out.println
        ("The head of the list is "+ls.getFirst());
    System.out.println
        ("The tail of the list is "+ls.getLast());
}
```

this gives rise to the display shown below:

```
List is [22, 300, 99, 100, 2, 3]
List is now [22, 300, 99, 100, 3]
The size of the list is 5
The head of the list is 22
The tail of the list is 3
```

8.3.4 Iterators

One of the major improvements in the Java 2 collection class over previous
versions is its provision of iterator objects. These are objects which are very

similar in concept to Enumeration objects. Their major difference is that they provide many more methods; they allow the programmer to carry out operations such as moving to the previous element which has been accessed and deleting the element which has just been processed. In the Java 2 collection classes there are two iterators: ListIterator and Iterator. The latter is the most similar to the Enumeration class in that it offers a method which checks that a collection of objects has been fully processed and a method which moves to the next object to be processed. There is, also, a method which removes an object. The three methods associated with Iterator objects are described below:

▸ next. This moves to the next element in a collection of objects.

▸ hasNext. This returns true if there is an object to be processed and false otherwise.

▸ remove. This removes the object which was returned by the last call of next.

The code below uses an Iterator object. It first sets up a HashSet with six elements which are integers and then creates an Iterator object it by sending the iterator message to the HashSet. This Iterator object is then used to traverse the HashSet collection. When an element less than 30 is encountered it is removed from the collection by means of the remove method.

```
public static void main(String[] args)
{
    HashSet hs = new HashSet();
    hs.add(new Integer(22));
    hs.add(new Integer(300));
    hs.add(new Integer(99));
    hs.add(new Integer(100));
    hs.add(new Integer(2));
    hs.add(new Integer(3));
    System.out.println("Set is "+hs);
    hs.remove(new Integer(2));
    //Set up iterator
    Iterator it = hs.iterator();
    System.out.println("Starting iteration");
    while(it.hasNext())
    {
        Integer val = (Integer)it.next();
        if(val.intValue()<30)
            //Delete element
            it.remove();
    }
    System.out.println("The set has become "+hs);
    System.out.println("The size of the set is "+hs.size());
}
```

This gives rise to the display:

```
Set is [100, 99, 300, 22, 3, 2]
Starting iteration
The set has become [100, 99, 300]
```

```
The size of the set is 3
```

The `ListIterator` interface extends the `Iterator` interface and provides further methods over and above those discussed above. The full list of methods are detailed below:

▶ `next`. Retrieves the next element in a collection.

▶ `nextIndex`. This returns the index of the element that will be returned by the next use of `next`.

▶ `previous`. This returns the previous element in a sequence.

▶ `hasNext`. This is true if there is a further element to process.

▶ `hasPrevious`. This is true if the use of `previous` will deliver an object.

▶ `previousIndex`. This returns the index of the object that is immediately before the one processed; it will return –1 if the current object is the first.

▶ `set`. This replaces the last object retrieved by either `next` or `previous` with its argument.

▶ `remove`. This removes the object which was retrieved by `next` or `previous`.

▶ `add`. This adds its argument before the object which would have been returned by the use of `next` and after the object that would be retrieved by `previous`.

The code below sets up a linked list implementation of a sequence with six integers. It then creates a `ListIterator` object `lit` which is used to iterate over the sequence. When an element is encountered which is greater than 30 it is replaced by an integer which is 200 greater than it.

```java
public static void main(String[] args)
{
    LinkedList ls = new LinkedList();
    ls.add(new Integer(122));
    ls.add(new Integer(200));
    ls.add(new Integer(919));
    ls.add(new Integer(88));
    ls.add(new Integer(21));
    ls.add(new Integer(13));
    System.out.println("List is "+ls);
    //Set up list iterator
    ListIterator lit = ls.listIterator();
    while(lit.hasNext())
    {
        Integer val = (Integer)lit.next();
        if(val.intValue()>30)
            //Replace element by one which is 200 greater
            lit.set(new Integer(val.intValue()+200));
```

```
    }
        System.out.println("The list has become "+ls);
}
```

The code below uses a `ListIterator` object `lit` to traverse a linked list implementation of a sequence containing six integers and then removes one of them and iterates down the list. When it encounters an element which is greater than 900 it deletes the element before the one encountered.

```
public static void main(String[] args)
{
    LinkedList ls = new LinkedList();
    ls.add(new Integer(2));
    ls.add(new Integer(200));
    ls.add(new Integer(919));
    ls.add(new Integer(88));
    ls.add(new Integer(21));
    ls.add(new Integer(13));
    System.out.println("List is "+ls);
    ls.remove(new Integer(2));
    //Set up a list iterator
    ListIterator lit = ls.listIterator();
    while(lit.hasNext())
    {
        Integer val = (Integer)lit.next();
        if(val.intValue()>900)
        {
            //Delete element
            lit.previous();
            lit.remove();
        }
    }
        System.out.println("The list has become "+ls);
}
```

The code assumes, of course, that the first element in the sequence is less than or equal to 900. The code gives rise to the display shown below:

```
List is [2, 200, 919, 88, 21, 13]
The list has become [919, 88, 21, 13]
```

8.4 Afterword

You would be forgiven wondering why, if there are now good class libaries which implement collections, the first third of the book has bothered to go into the detail of how collections are implemented. After all, the class libraries detailed in this chapter are readily available and all a programmer has to do is to import the library and use the collections that he or she requires. The reason why the book went into such detail in its first third is because the user of a collection class library needs to know something of the properties of a particular implementation—such as how much memory is used and how fast it will be—before they can make an informed choice about which class to use.

CHAPTER SUMMARY

▶ There are now a number of sophisticated class libraries that implement collections.

▶ One of the earliest and best is the JGL class library.

▶ Java 2 also has a good class library which implements many of the collections described in the first third of the book.

▶ Such class libraries enable the developer to eliminate the sort of detailed programming described in the first third of the book.

Larger Class Examples

This chapter:

▸ Demonstrates the use of inheritance and aggregation using examples larger than those previously described.
▸ Describes some realistic collections of data.

In this chapter you will meet, for the first time, some collections which are close to those found in real, industrial systems.

9.1 Introduction

The previous chapters have described a large number of classes that represent collections such as sets and sequences. This chapter describes how such classes can be combined together in order to construct more application-oriented systems. The aim of this section is to give you a feel for how classes can be combined and, in particular, the two mechanisms which are used in patterns: aggregation and inheritance.

9.2 Some small examples

In order to show the use of inheritance and aggregation this section and the next will describe class implementations which attempt to save on either space or time. Programmers are often faced with an application where the data has some property which enables them to develop a more efficient implementation than would be allowed if they used the classes in a class library directly. In the next subsections I will examine how we can take advantage of data properties and use inheritance and aggregtion to build efficient classes.

9.2.1 The frequently accessed object

A number of applications have the property that over a period of time only one object is manipulated. For example, when using the word processor for this book I tended to work on the file containing the current chapter for a period of three to four days, very rarely did I open any other. Let us assume that we wish to develop a singly linked list class which can respond to the same methods as the JGL Slist class but which is optimised to take advantage of the fact that one object will be retrieved very frequently over a period of time. The implementation of this class is shown below

```
class SingleList extends SList{

private Object popular;

SingleList()
{
super(); popular = null;
}

public boolean contains (Object o)
{
if (o.equals(popular))
    return true;
else
{
   popular = o;
   return super.contains(o);
}
}

}
```

The class inherits from Slist so all the methods of that class are available to any user of SingleList. In implementing the class I have assumed that the method contains will be executed a very large number of times with the same argument. The class has an instance variable popular which contains the value of the last object looked up using the method contains. This will normally be equal to the most popular object. The code for contains first checks that the argument is equal to the most popular object looked up. If it isn't then the contains method within Slist is executed and popular is updated.

9.2.2 The sparse array

The previous implementations have been of a class which use extra memory in a search for greater speed. The example in this section attempts to save memory.

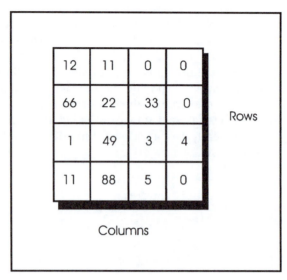

Figure 9.1 A two-dimensional array

An array is a two-dimensional structure used by mathematicians. An example of a typical two-dimensional array with four rows and four columns is shown in Figure 9.1.

There is a branch of mathematics known as numerical analysis that uses arrays to store numbers that are used in the approximate numerical solution of sets of equations. Often these arrays are sparse: they contain few elements; for example, the array might have 10 rows and 10 columns and yet only contain five elements. A conventional implementation of such an array would waste rather a lot of space and there is a need for some implementation which minimises the waste. In this section I shall look at a fast implementation where some space is wasted.

The implementation I shall use is that of a JGL `HashMap` which maps a (row, column) pair to the object that is stored at that location. This implementation will be fast since it is based on hashing; however, it does require some redundant space since hashing only works when a high proportion of the space in the table is empty. However, the overall space required is usually much less than if the sparse array were implemented directly. The class describing this implementation consists of 5 methods:

▶ A constructor which has two arguments that represent the largest row and column numbers in the array.

▶ `getVal` which returns with the value stored at a position in the array given by a row and column number.

▶ `setVal` which stores an object at a particular row and column.

▶ `getRows` which retrieves the number of rows in the array.

▶ `getColumns` which retrieves the number of columns in the array.

The class skeleton that describes row–column combinations is shown below. Most of the methods are straightforward. Notice, however, that three methods toString, hashCode and equals are provided. toString turns an object into a string and is useful for debugging using System.out. hashCode generates an integer[1] used to access the HashMap into which the array objects are stored and equals is used by the get and put methods of HashMap in order to locate a particular object stored in it. All these methods override defaults which are associated with the class Object. In the case of hashCode we have used a simple calculation which involves multiplying the row number by 100 and adding the column number to it.

```
class RowColumn{

private int column;
private int row;

public boolean equals(Object o)
{
RowColumn b = (RowColumn) o;
return
   (getColumn() == b.getColumn() && getRow() == b.getRow());
}

public RowColumn(int rw, int cl)
{
row = rw;
column = cl;
}

public String toString()
{
return "RowColumn("+row+" , "+column+")";
}

public int hashCode()
{
return row*100 + column;
}

public int getColumn()
{
return column;
}

public int getRow()
{
return row;
```

---

[1] This is the method which works out the position of an object in a HashMap; it does this in exactly the same way that I described in Chapter 4 where a calculation determined the first potential position of an object in a set.

```
}

}
```

Most of the code for the class used to implement the sparse two-dimensional array is shown below. The methods setVal and getVal throw two exceptions RowException and ColumnException if an attempt is made to access the array past its row or column bounds.

```
class TwoDArray{

private HashMap array;
private int maxColumn;
private int maxRow;

public TwoDArray(int nmRows,int nmColumns)
{
maxColumn = nmColumns; maxRow = nmRows;
array = new HashMap();
}

public void setVal(int row, int column, Object o)
    throws RowException, ColumnException
{
//Code for setVal that sets the element identified by
//row and column to be the value o.
}

public Object getVal(int row, int col)
    throws RowException, ColumnException
{
Object o;
if (row>maxRow)
   throw new RowException();
if (col >maxColumn)
   throw new ColumnException();
o = array.get(new RowColumn(row,col));
return o;
}

public int getColumns()
{
return maxColumn;
}

public int getRows()
{
return maxRow;
}

}
```

SELF TEST QUESTION 1

Write down the code for the method setVal. Assume that it throws a RowException or a ColumnException if the arguments are out of range.

9.3 Larger examples

This section describes two further examples of large data types; in contrast to the examples detailed previously they are taken from specific Internet applications and use facilities from the JGL class library.

9.3.1 An electronic mailing list manager

Electronic mail has overtaken postal mail as the medium for information transfer in my life. In this I am no different from many other computer users. I am registered on a number of mailing lists which regularly provide me with important information that I need to function as an academic. For example, I belong to a mailing list which regularly sends out information to its subscribers about developments affecting the Java programming language. I am also a member of a departmental mailing list which is used to send messages about my academic department. There are a number of utilities in existence that administer mailing lists, some of these are simple and are provided as part of an operating system, some are quite complex and are used to administer mailing lists with tens of thousands of users. Later in the book in Chapters 12 and 13 I will look at a more elegant implementation of a mailing list using a concept known as a pattern.

This subsection looks at the data used to support a large mailing list. I shall assume that subscribers will subscribe to this mailing list by sending a message such as

```
subscribe Darrel Ince
```

to such a list. The manager will then obtain the email address of the user from the email header and enter the name of the subscriber together with their email address in the list. I shall also assume that the mailing list will be split up into a number of different subgroups which have an interest in a particular topic. For example, if a mailing list contained subscribers who were interested in issues affecting the accounting, sales and support functions of a company, then assignment to a group is done by the user appending a second line to the email message above such as

```
Groups Accounts Sales Support
```

I will also assume that some subscribers will not be interested in belonging to a particular group but are only interested in receiving general messages. There will be two types of message sent from the mailing list: first, there will be messages sent to the subscribers; second, messages sent to every subscriber irrespective of whether they are registered with any groups.

The operations that will be implemented are:

▶ An operation which registers a user as a subscriber to the mailing list.

▶ An operation which registers a user as a member of a group of the mailing list.

▶ An operation which removes a user as a subscriber. The user will be removed from every group that he or she belongs to and all their details will be removed.

▶ An operation which removes a subscriber from a particular group.

▶ An operation which creates a new group.

▶ An operation which deletes an existing group.

▶ An operation which returns with the number of subscribers who are currently registered with the system.

▶ An operation which returns with the number of subscribers associated with a particular group.

▶ An operation which, given two user-groups, returns with the collection of users who are members of both groups.

It is worth stressing at this stage that the system I have described contains only a limited number of operations. Real mailing list administration systems contain further facilities for carrying out functions such as determining when a subscriber's email address is no longer valid and for keeping track of the emails that have been sent out.

Figure 9.2 shows the architecture of the data used for this system. It consist of a number of collections:

▶ The first represents individual subscribers. A subscriber is represented by a name and an email address.

Figure 9.2 the architecture of a mailing system

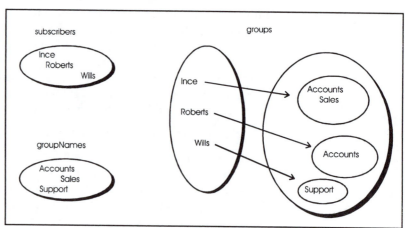

▶ There is a collection of group names corresponding to mailing lists. This is modelled as a set.

▶ There is an association between a group and the collection of subscribers who make up that group. This is modelled by a map which relates the name of the group to a set of subscribers.

The code skeleton for the class that describes email users is shown below.

```java
public class EmailUser{

private String  name,          //Name of the user
                emailAddress;  //The email address
                               //of the user

EmailUser(String name, String emailAddress)
{
    this.name = name;
    this.emailAddress = emailAddress;
}


public String getName()
{
    return name;
}

public void setName(String name)
{
    this.name = name;
}

public String getEmailAddress()
{
    return emailAddress;
}

public void setAddress(String emailAddress)
{
    this.emailAddress = emailAddress;
}

public String toString()
{
    return "User = "+ name+" address = "+ emailAddress+"\n";
}

public boolean equals(Object o)
{
    EmailUser  ev = (EmailUser)o;
    return ev.name == name &&
           ev.emailAddress == emailAddress;
```

```
}

public int hashCode()
{
    return emailAddress.hashCode()+name.hashCode();
}

}
```

The only point worth mentioning about this class occurs with the method hashCode which uses the built-in method hashCode of the String class to define an overall hash value for the EmailUser class.

The code skeleton for the EmailSystem class is shown below. Any errors cause the creation of an IllegalArgumentException object.

```
public class EmailSystem{

//subscribers contains the global list of subscribers
//groupNames contains the strings which designate
//each of the mailing groups
//groups maps a group name to a set containing
//all the members of the group

private HashSet    subscribers,
                   groupNames;
private HashMap    groups;

EmailSystem()
{
groups = new HashMap();
subscribers = new HashSet();
groupNames = new HashSet();
}

public void registerUser(EmailUser eu)throws
IllegalArgumentException
{
//Registers eu as a subscriber
}

public void registerUserToGroup(EmailUser eu, String  gp)
                      throws IllegalArgumentException
{
//Registers the user eu with the group gp
}

public void removeAll(EmailUser eu)throws
IllegalArgumentException
{
//Removes the user eu from all subscribed groups
}

public void removeFromGroup(EmailUser eu, String gp)
                      throws IllegalArgumentException
{
```

```
//Removes the user eu from the group gp
}

public void createGroup(String gp)throws
IllegalArgumentException
{
//Creates a new group gp
}

public void deleteGroup(String gp)throws
IllegalArgumentException
{
//Deletes the group gp
}

public int returnNoSubscribers()
{
//Returns with the number of subscribers
}

public int returnNoInGroup(String gp)throws
IllegalArgumentException
{
//Returns with the number of subscribers to the group gp
}

public HashSet allInBoth(String gp1, String gp2)
                throws IllegalArgumentException
{
//Returns with the set containing all the users who
//are in both the group gp1 and gp2
}

}
```

SELF TEST QUESTION 2

Write down the code for the method `registerUser`. Assume that it throws an `IllegalArgumentException` if the user is already registered. You will need to use the `HashSet` method `add` which adds an object to a `HashSet` object and returns `null` if the object was not already in the set.

The next method is `registerUserToGroup` which registers a user to a particular group. It makes use of the method `count` which counts the number of members in a set which match its argument. It also makes use of `get` and `put` which are the analogues of `get` and `put` found in `Hashtable`.

```
public void registerUserToGroup(EmailUser eu, String  gp)
                        throws IllegalArgumentException
{
```

```
if (groups.count(gp)!=1)
    throw new IllegalArgumentException
                    ("Group does not exist");
//User must already be registered
if (subscribers.count(eu)!=1)
    throw new IllegalArgumentException
                    ("User not registered");
else
{
    HashSet val = (HashSet)groups.get(gp);
    if(val.count(eu)==1)
        throw new IllegalArgumentException
            ("User already registered with group");
    val.add(eu);
    groups.put(gp,val);
}
}
```

The next method is `removeAll`. This removes a subscriber and his or her membership of all the mailing groups.

```
public void removeAll(EmailUser eu)throws
IllegalArgumentException
{
if (subscribers.count(eu)!=1)
    throw new IllegalArgumentException
                ("User not registered");
Enumeration e = groups.elements();
while(e.hasMoreElements())
{
    HashSet val = (HashSet)e.nextElement();
    if(val.count(eu)==1)
        val.remove(eu);
}
subscribers.remove(eu);
}
```

It does this by retrieving an enumeration which represents all the collections of users associated with each group and then removing the user from each of those which he or she is associated with; finally the user is removed from the general subscription list.

SELF TEST QUESTION 3

Write down the code for the method `removeFromGroup`. Assume that it throws an `IllegalArgumentException` if the group does not exist or the user has not been registered. The method takes two arguments, the first is a string which is the user, the second is also a string but represents the group.

The methods `createGroup` and `deleteGroup` create a group and delete a group respectively:

```
public void createGroup(String gp)throws
IllegalArgumentException
{
if (groups.count(gp)!=0)
    throw new IllegalArgumentException
                ("Group already exists");
groups.put(gp,new HashSet());
groupNames.add(gp);
}

public void deleteGroup(String gp)throws
IllegalArgumentException
{
if (groups.count(gp)!=1)
    throw new IllegalArgumentException
                ("Group does not exist");
groups.remove(gp);
groupNames.remove(gp);
}
```

The methods `returnNoSubscribers` and `returnNoInGroup` return numerical information. The former returns with the total number of subscribers, the latter returns with the number of subscribers associated with a particular group.

```
public int returnNoSubscribers()
{
return subscribers.size();
}

public int returnNoInGroup(String gp)throws
IllegalArgumentException
{
if (groups.count(gp)!=1)
    throw new IllegalArgumentException
                ("Group does not exist");
HashSet hs = (HashSet)groups.get(gp);
return hs.size();
}
```

Finally, the method `allInBoth` returns with the set which contains all the users who are contained in the groups which are its arguments. It uses the method `union` which returns with the collection of members in the set formed from the common members in its argument and the destination object.

SELF TEST QUESTION 4

Write down the code for the method `allInBoth`. The method takes two arguments which are groups and it returns with a `HashSet` which contains all the users who are members of both groups. The method will throw an `IllegalArgumentException` if the groups are are not recognised.

9.3.2 Data for a search engine

Search engines are programs which contain massive indexes to the documents on the Internet, these documents usually reside on the World Wide Web or are part of postings to USENET user groups. There are a number of search engines, most of which are free. Someone wishing to find some documents on the Internet will first set their browser to point at the home page of the search engine and then type in a query. Some search engines allow natural language queries; all of them allow a restricted form of query framed in some heavily constrained search language. For example, the Alta Vista search engine will let the user type in a query such as

```
Compiler AND Java
```

which will return with hyperlinks to all those documents which contain the words *Java* and *Compiler*. At the heart of a search engine is a set of massive indexes and the aim of this section is to look at a simplified set of collections which could support the storage and querying of these indexes. Before looking at the code it is worth saying that the code is rather simple; for example, most of the code used in such search engines has the function of manipulating data held on files while the code presented here assumes that the indexes are stored in memory. However, most of the principles outlined in this section are the same.

Figure 9.3 shows how a search engine index could be modelled using a map which maps words in an index to the files containing the html documents in which the word is contained. Each word is mapped to a set of document identifiers.

Two operations are required for this system:

▶ An operation which adds a new word associated with a particular document.

▶ An operation which, given a query consisting of a pattern of words including *and* operators and *or* operators, returns with the documents that satisfy the query.

In the code presented below I have assumed that queries will consist of words separated by either a + (for and) or | (for or). I have made the simplifying assumption that both the words and the operators are always separated by space. The code also carries out no error processing.

SELF TEST QUESTION 5

What instance variables would be needed for a class which implemented the storage for a search engine?

The code for the class is shown below:

```
class SearchData {
private HashMap associations;
SearchData()
{
associations = new HashMap();
}

public void addAssociation(String word, String address)
{
HashSet hs;
if(associations.count(word)>0)
    hs = (HashSet)associations.get(word);
else
    hs = new HashSet();
hs.add(address);
associations.put(word,hs);
}

public HashSet retrieve(String pattern)
{
//Sets up a string tokenizer on the search string
//the terminator for substrings in the search string
//is white space
StringTokenizer st = new StringTokenizer(pattern);
HashSet temp = new HashSet();
while (st.hasMoreTokens())
{
    //Get next substring terminated by white space
    String nextString = st.nextToken();
    if((!nextString.equals("+"))&&(!nextString.equals("|")))
       temp=temp.union
           ((HashSet)associations.get(nextString));
    else
       if(nextString.equals("+"))
       {
          nextString = st.nextToken();
          HashSet foundSet
               =(HashSet)associations.get(nextString);
          temp =temp.intersection(foundSet);
       }
       else
          if(nextString.equals("|"))
          {
             nextString = st.nextToken();
             HashSet foundSet =
                 (HashSet)associations.get(nextString);
             temp=temp.union(foundSet);
          }
}
return temp;}

}
```

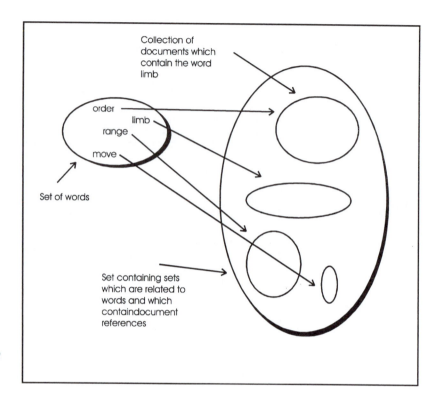

Collection of
documents which
contain the word
limb

order

limb

range

move

Set of words

Set containing sets
which are related to
words and which
containdocument
references

Figure 9.3
Storage for a
Web search

There are two methods in this class. The instance variable `associations` is a map from a word to a set of documents which contain the word.

The first method `addAssociation` processes a word which is its first argument and the name of a Web document which is its second argument. It first checks if there is already an association. If there is it just adds the document name to the collection of document names associated with the word, if there isn't then it sets up a new set to contain the documents and then adds the word to it.

The second method `retrieve` takes a string which is a query framed in terms of +, – and search words. It loops around merging sets (via the `union` method) or finding common members of two sets (via the `intersection` method). The method makes use of an object known as a `StringTokenizer`. This allows access to the substrings of a string which are terminated by a nominated string. This nominated string is usually communicated to the `StringTokenizer` via a constructor. In the example above the default one-argument `StringTokenizer` constructor is used, this employs the space default string. The method `nextToken` will return the next string in a substring which is terminated by the terminating string; in the case above this is white space. The method `hasMoreTokens` is true as long as there are some substrings to process.

CHAPTER SUMMARY

▸ Larger collections of data are constructed using inheritance and aggregation.

▸ For larger collections of data large number of classes are usually employed rather than the single class implementations shown previously.

Implementing Graphs

This chapter:

▶ Describes the graph abstract data type.
▶ Shows how graphs can be implemented in a number of ways.
▶ Describes a number of complex graph algorithms.
▶ Introduces a number of vocabulary terms associated with graphs.
▶ Provides further examples of the development of large classes.

This chapter is the last one to look at a particular abstract data type. It is distinguished from previous chapters in that the degree of programming complexity is higher.

graph – an abstract data type containing data objects which are connected to each other

edge – a join between two vertices in a graph

vertex – an element of a graph

directed graph – a graph where the relationship between vertices has directionality

10.1 Introduction

This chapter discusses a collection known as a graph and will describe a number of implementations. You may be thinking that this chapter is a little out of place in the book: it should, perhaps, directly follow on from the chapters which discuss the implementation of sets, sequences and maps, or even form part of the chapter which described modern class libraries. The reason it is placed here is that it draws on facilities found in these class libraries for implementation, and also the fact that the class libraries I have discussed have yet to get around to implementing graph classes. A graph consists of a number of nodes which are connected to other nodes. An example of a graph is shown in Figure 10.1. It consists of entities known as vertices which contain data, and links between these vertices known as edges. A graph where directionality is important and indicated by arrowed edges is known as a directed graph.

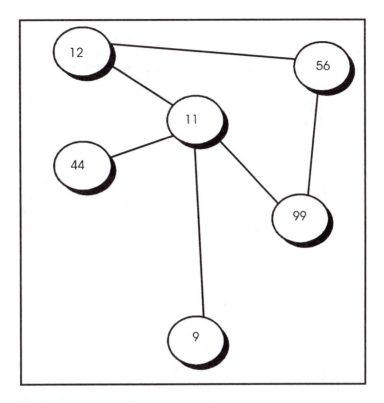

**Figure 10.1
An example of
a graph**

When a vertex is connected to another vertex we say that it is incident to the second vertex, so 44 is incident to 11 in Figure 10.1. The degree of a vertex is the number of edges which emerge from it. A path in a graph is a sequence of nodes that are connected together. An example of a path in

GLOSSARY

degree – the degree
of a vertex is the
number of edges
which emerge from it

incident – when a
vertex is connected to
another vertex in a
graph we say that it is
incident to it

path – is a series of
vertices which are
connected to each
other

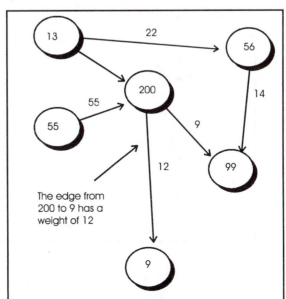

**Figure 10.2 A
weighted
directed
graph**

Figure 10.1 is 12, 11, 44.

A path is termed simple if it doesn't contain any duplicate vertices. The length of a path is the number of edges in the path; for example, the length of the path 12, 11, 44 in Figure 10.1 is 2. A graph is connected if all the vertices in the graph are connected by paths.

A loop in a graph is a sequence of paths which start at one vertex and end up at the same vertex. A graph which has no loops is known as a tree.

One important type of graph which crops up frequently in computer applications is a weighted graph. This consists of a graph where the vertices are associated with a weighting value. For example, if the graph represents the connections in a road system then the weight might represent the distance in km between towns (which are the vertices). An example of a weighted graph is shown in Figure 10.2.

Graphs are an important collection class and crop up in some computationally demanding applications. For example, they can be used to model:

▶ The connections between computers in a network. Data based on graphs can be used to calculate the paths a message can take through the network.

▶ The connections between cities and towns. Applications which involve the scheduling of deliveries by freight carriers rely on software which accesses a model of the road network implemented as a graph.

The connections in an electronic circuit. Computer-aided design software which helps VLSI designers built up circuit diagrams relies on the circuit topology being modelled as a graph.

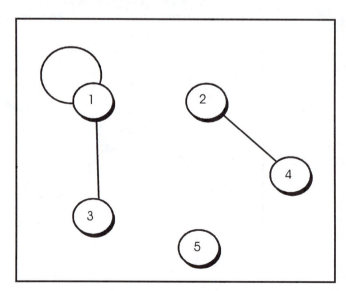

Figure 10.3 Another example of a graph

10.2 Implementation

There are a number of ways of implementing graphs. The first is by using a
two-dimensional array. A simple version of this is shown in Figure 10.4
which shows the implementation of the graph in Figure 10.3. Here the
elements of the graph are Booleans. If an element j,k of the graph is false
then there is no link between the nodes j and k; however, if the value of j,k
is true then there is a link. Links are stored symmetrically in that if there is
an entry that describes that node j is connected to node k, then there will
be an entry which specifies that that node k is connected to node j. In
Figure 10.4 the false entries are not shown.

SELF TEST QUESTION 1

What are two criticisms of this implementation?

Before looking at some code it is worth addressing the first problem
described in the answer to the self test question above. A slightly more
complicated implementation is shown in Figure 10.5. Here the array is
combined with a table that maps objects of class `Object` to numbers
which range from 1 to some upper limit. This provides a mapping from
any object to the element of the graph.

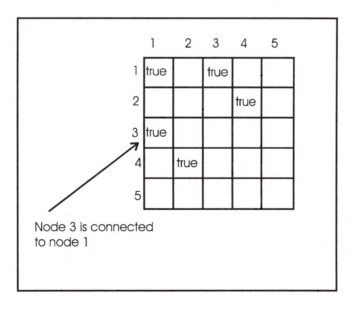

*Figure 10.4 The
implementation
of the graph
shown in Figure
10.3*

Node 3 is connected
to node 1

The skeleton code for a graph class that implements this form of organisation and which contains the following operations is shown below:

▶ A constructor which sets up the basic data for the class. The constructor has a single int argument that gives the upper limits of the array.

▶ A method which adds an edge to the graph, the edge being distinguished by its vertices.

▶ A method which deletes an edge from the graph, the edge being distinguished by its vertices.

▶ A method which returns true if there is a connection between two vertices.

▶ A method which returns with the degree of a vertex.

▶ A method which adds a vertex to the graph.

No error processing is included in the code.

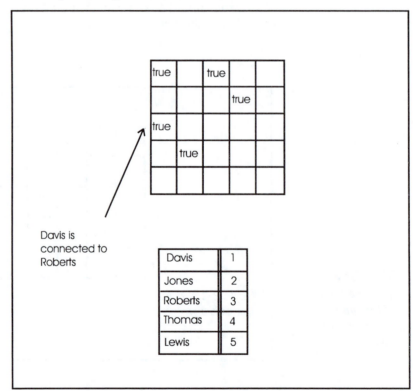

Davis is connected to Roberts

Figure 10.5 A more complicated implementation of a graph.

```
class ArrayGraph {

private  boolean[][]      links;         //Contains edges
private Hashtable        nodeNames;      //Maps vertex names
private int noOfVertices,  size;         //No of vertices

public ArrayGraph(int n)
{
size = n;
for (int i = 0;i<size;i++)
{
   //Set all the elements of links false
   links[i] = new boolean[5];
   for(int j = 0;j<size;j++)
      links[i][j] = false;
}
nodeNames = new Hashtable();
//No vertices stored at present
noOfVertices = 0;
}

public void addLink(Object vertex1, Object vertex2)
{
//Code for addLink
}

public void deleteLink(Object vertex1, Object vertex2)
{
//Code for deleteLink
}

public boolean isLink(Object vertex1, Object vertex2)
{
//Code for isLink
}

public int degree(Object vertex)
{
//Code for degree
}

public void addVertex(Object vertex)
{
//Code for addVertex
}
}
```

The code for the constructor just initialises the Boolean array holding the link information and sets up the hash table and two instance variables which hold the size of the array and a count of the number of vertices in the graph.

The code for the method addLink which takes two vertices as its arguments and then establishes a link between them is shown below:

```
public void addLink(Object vertex1, Object vertex2)
```

```
{
   int index1=0, index2=0;
   Integer n1 = (Integer)nodeNames.get(vertex1),
           n2 = (Integer)nodeNames.get(vertex2);
   if(n1==null)
   {
      //Name of vertex not found
      index1 = noOfVertices;
      nodeNames.put(vertex1, new Integer(noOfVertices));
      noOfVertices++;
   }
   if(n2 ==null)
   {
      //Name of vertex not found
      index2 = noOfVertices;
      nodeNames.put(vertex2, new Integer(noOfVertices));
      noOfVertices++;
   }
   links[index1][index2] = links[index2][index1] = true;
}
```

It first checks that the two vertices are already in the graph; if not then it adds an entry into the nodeNames table which relates the vertices to their index in the Boolean array links which keeps link information. After this processing has occurred links is updated to show the new link; since the array is symmetrical two entries in it are set to true. Notice that objects defined by Integer are stored in the HashMap since such collections can only store objects.

SELF TEST QUESTION 2

Write down the code for deleteLink.

The code for the method isLink is shown below:

```
public boolean isLink(Object vertex1, Object vertex2)

{
   int index1, index2;
   index1 = ((Integer)nodeNames.get(vertex1)).intValue();
   index2 = ((Integer)nodeNames.get(vertex2)).intValue();
   return links[index1][index2];
}
```

It returns with a true or false value depending on whether the Boolean array links indicates a link between the two vertices.

SELF TEST QUESTION 3

The method degree returns with an int value which is the number of vertices connected to the object which is its argument. Write down the code for this method.

The full code of the class is shown below including the simple method
addVertex.

```
class ArrayGraph {

private  boolean[][]     links;
private Hashtable        nodeNames;
int noOfVertices,        size;

ArrayGraph(int n)
{
size = n;
for (int i = 0;i<size;i++)
{
   //Set all the links false since there are no vertices
   links[i] = new boolean[5];
   for(int j = 0;j<size;j++)
      links[i][j] = false;
}
nodeNames = new Hashtable();
//No vertices yet
noOfVertices = 0;
}

public void addLink(Object vertex1, Object vertex2)
{
int index1=0, index2=0;
Integer n1 = (Integer)nodeNames.get(vertex1),
        n2 = (Integer)nodeNames.get(vertex2);
if(n1 ==null)
{
   //Create a new vertex
   index1 = noOfVertices;
   nodeNames.put(vertex1, new Integer(noOfVertices));
   noOfVertices++;
}
if(n2 ==null)
{
   //Create a new vertex
   index2 = noOfVertices;
   nodeNames.put(vertex2, new Integer(noOfVertices));
   noOfVertices++;
}
links[index1][index2] = links[index2][index1] = true;
}

public void deleteLink(Object vertex1, Object vertex2)
{
int index1, index2;
index1 = ((Integer)nodeNames.get(vertex1)).intValue();
index2 = ((Integer)nodeNames.get(vertex2)).intValue();
links[index1][index2] = links[index2][index1] = false;
}

public boolean isLink(Object vertex1, Object vertex2)
{
```

```
int index1, index2;
index1 = ((Integer)nodeNames.get(vertex1)).intValue();
index2 = ((Integer)nodeNames.get(vertex2)).intValue();
return links[index1][index2];
}

public int degree(Object vertex)
{
int index, count=0;
index = ((Integer)nodeNames.get(vertex)).intValue();
//Move down a row counting links
for(int j = 0;j<size;j++)
   if(links[index][j])
       count++;
return count;
}

public void addVertex(Object vertex)
{
nodeNames.put(vertex, new Integer(noOfVertices));
noOfVertices++;
}

}
```

SELF TEST QUESTION 4

What if you wanted to implement a method that deletes a vertex from the graph. Would this require a lot of extra work?

An alternative implementation to the Boolean array implementation which potentially uses less space is shown in Figure 10.6.
Here the graph is expressed as a map from a vertex to the collection of objects which are connected to that vertex. The map is implemented in terms of a Java `Hashtable` while the collection of connected objects is implemented in terms of a `Vector`.

10.3 Some complicated operations

The previous section described some rather simple operations. The aim of this section is to show much more complicated operations that are often needed in a graph package.

10.3.1 Breadth first search

A breadth first search of a graph starts with a particular vertex often called the distinguished vertex of the graph and then determines all the vertices in the graph that are reachable from this vertex; it also usually applies some operation to each of the vertices that have been found.

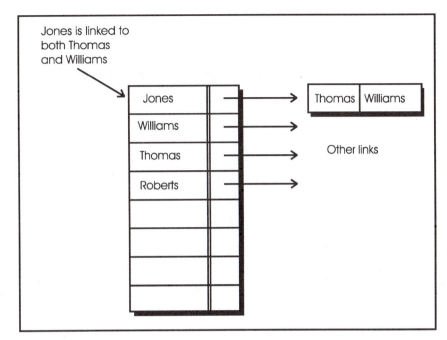

Jones is linked to
both Thomas
and Williams

Jones | | → | Thomas | Williams

Williams | | →

Thomas | | → Other links

Roberts | | →

Figure 10.6
Another
implementation
of a graph

The term *breadth first search* is so named because it searches on level by
level through the vertices for all those that are connected. The code for this
search is shown below. However, before looking at it in detail it is worth
examining the implementation of a weighted graph that is to be described
in this section. It is shown below:

```
public class Graph{

private HashSet      vertices;
private HashSet      edges;
private HashMap      weights;

Graph()
{
vertices = new HashSet();
edges = new HashSet();
weights = new HashMap();
}

}
```

The instance variables all employ JGL collections. The collection of vertices
is held in the set `vertices`, the edges of the graph are held in the set
`edges` and a map `weights` maps an edge to its weight.

SELF TEST QUESTION 5

What criticism would you make of this implementation?

The class that implements edges in the graph is shown below:

```
class Edge {
private Object first, second;

Edge(Object first, Object second)
{
this.first = first;
this.second = second;
}

public Object getFirst()
{
return first;
}

public Object getSecond()
{
return second;
}

public int hashCode()
{
return first.hashCode()+second.hashCode();
}

public String toString()
{
return "( "+ first.toString()  + "   " +second.toString()+
       " )"+"\n";
}

public boolean equals(Object o)
{
return (((Edge)o).first).equals(first) &&
       (((Edge)o).second).equals(second);
}

}
```

SELF TEST QUESTION 6

Why does this implementation contain the methods `equals`, `toString` and `hashCode`?

Given the class `Graph` and the class `Edge`, the code for the depth first search can be presented. It uses recursion to carry out the traversal of the graph.

```
public void visitAndDo(AppObjectProcess ao)
{
HashMap visited = new HashMap();
Enumeration e = vertices.elements();
while(e.hasMoreElements())
{
    Object o = e.nextElement();
```

```
        visited.put(o, new Boolean(false));
    }
//Reset enumeration
e = vertices.elements();
while(e.hasMoreElements())
{
    Object o = e.nextElement();
     if(!(((Boolean)visited.get(o)).booleanValue()))
       //Has not been visited, so visit it
       moveOver(o,visited, ao);

}
}

private void moveOver
       (Object o, HashMap hm, AppObjectProcess ao)
{
Enumeration h = vertices.elements();
hm.put(o, new Boolean(true));
//Apply the operation
ao.apply(o);
while(h.hasMoreElements())
{
    Object ho = h.nextElement();
    //Check if there is a edge
    if(weights.count(new Edge(o,ho))==1||
       weights.count(new Edge(ho,o))==1)
       if (!((Boolean)hm.get(o)).booleanValue())
         moveOver(ho,hm,ao);
}
}
```

The method that is used by the programmer is visitAndDo which makes use of the private helper method moveOver. The former uses a HashMap visited to keep track of the vertices that have been visited. The vertices are first enumerated, then each of them is marked as not having been visited. Then, the method loops over the enumeration checking whether each vertex has been visited, if it hasn't then the method moveOver is applied, this travels over the vertices that are linked to the one being considered.

moveOver marks the vertex as visited and then sequentially examines each edge key in the HashMap object weights to check for connections and then recursively applies itself to any connected vertices.

The method apply takes an object defined by the interface AppObjectProcess and applies the method apply defined in this class. This method will embed any functionality required to be applied to a vertex. The code for this interface is shown below:

```
public interface AppObjectProcess{

public void apply(Object o);

}

}
```

SELF TEST QUESTION 7

If you wanted the process to be applied to each vertex to be the display of each vertex on `System.out` what code would be needed?

10.3.2 Constructing a minimum spanning tree

A minimum spanning tree of a weighted graph *g* is a graph which is a tree and which is a subgraph of *g* where the total weight of all the vertices of the tree is a minimum.

One application for a minimum spanning tree algorithm is finding the minimum amount of wiring required in a circuit so that each element of the circuit is connected. The circuit being modelled by a weighted graph, where the vertices represent the wiring and the weights represent the length of wire used.

There are a number of algorithms which, given a weighted graph, produce the minimum spanning tree. They all work by gradually starting with a collection of subsets of the graph which are trees; these are then coalesced to a smaller number of subsets containing a larger number of vertices, where each subset is still a tree. A vertex that has been added to a subset of the minimum spanning tree is known as a safe vertex. Eventually there will only be one tree left, this is the minimum spanning tree. Each set is disjoint: that is no two sets contain common pairs.

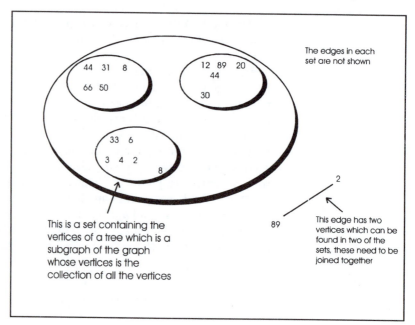

Figure 10.7 One step in Kruskal's algorithm

The algorithm that is presented in this subsection is due to Kruskal. It uses the implementation of a weighted graph described in the previous section. What Kruskal's algorithm does is to initially create a number of simple trees which just contain a single vertex. The initial number of trees will be the number of vertices in the weighted directed graph that is to be processed. Next, the edges of the graph are stored in order of increasing weight. A loop then checks each vertex in this order to see whether the vertices which make up each edge can be found in the same tree. If they do then they are discarded since adding them to an existing tree creates a cycle and destroys the tree property (Remember that a tree is a special form of graph which has no cycles). If the vertices are in different trees then both these trees are joined together to form a larger tree.

Eventually all the subtrees will have been joined together to form a single tree which is the minimum spanning tree. This is an example of a greedy algorithm where a sophisticated search of vertices in increasing order yields a minimum spanning tree. Figure 10.7 shows one step in the algorithm.

In order to describe the algorithm it is first necessary to describe a collection known as a disjoint set. Such a set contains a collection of sets which have the property that none of the sets share common elements. An example of such a set is shown in Figure 10.8.

The code for a disjoint set is shown below.

```
class DisjointSet{

private HashMap mapper;

DisjointSet()
{
mapper = new HashMap();
}

public void add(Object o)
{
mapper.put(o,o);
}

public void union(Object first, Object second)
{
//Forms the union of the two disjoint sets first
//and second within the collection mapper
Object firstDistinguished = mapper.get(first),
       secondDistinguished = mapper.get(second);
Enumeration e = mapper.keys();
while(e.hasMoreElements())
{
  Object key = e.nextElement();
  if(mapper.get(key).equals(secondDistinguished))
    mapper.put(key,firstDistinguished);
}
}
```

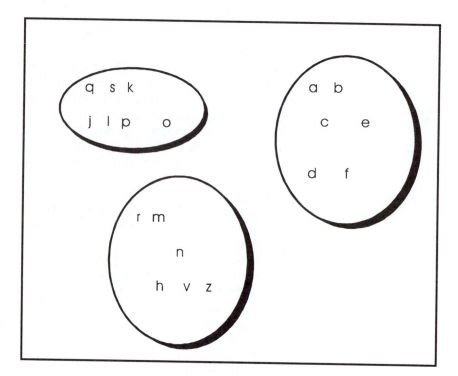

*Figure 10.8 A
disjoint set*

```
public Object distinguished(Object o)
{
return mapper.get(o);
}


}
```

The class uses a JGL `HashMap` to implement the disjoint set; it maps each element in the disjoint set to a representative element, where a representative element is any element of the set. This is shown as Figure 10.9.

There are three methods within the class; `add` creates a single set which contains its argument; `union` joins two sets within the disjoint set together, and `distinguished` returns the nominated distinguished element of a set.

Given this implementation of the disjoint set we can now outline Kruskal's algorithm. The first lines declare all the objects needed:

```
public HashSet Kruskal()
{
SList edgeList = new SList();
DisjointSet ds= new DisjointSet();
HashSet a = new HashSet();
```

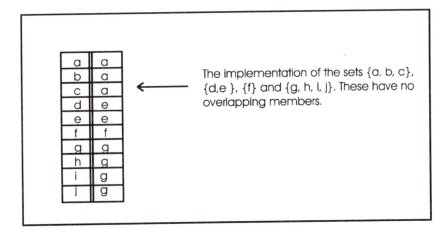

The implementation of the sets {a, b, c}, {d,e }, {f} and {g, h, i, j}. These have no overlapping members.

Figure 10.9 The implementation of the disjoint set

A disjoint set `ds` is needed to hold the vertices which represent subgraphs (trees) that have the disjoint property; the set `a` is used to build up the vertices which are identified as belonging to the minimum spanning tree; the linked list `edgeList` is used to hold the vertices of the graph which is to be processed in order of increasing weight.

The next lines of code creates a disjoint set which contains singleton sets that are the vertices of the graph to be processed.

```
Enumeration e = vertices.elements();
while(e.hasMoreElements())
{
Object vertex = e.nextElement();
ds.add(vertex);
}
```

Next the edges are added to a singly linked list which is then sorted in order of increasing weight.

```
e = edges.elements();
while(e.hasMoreElements())
    edgeList.pushBack(e.nextElement());
Sorting.sort(edgeList, new IntComparator(weights));
```

The method `pushBack` places each edge into the singly linked list and then the JGL static method `Sorting.sort` carries out the sorting. In order to do this it requires an object which implements the JGL interface `BinaryPredicate`. This carries out the comparison of adjacent elements in the list in order to determine their position. The code for the class `IntComparator` is shown below

```
class IntComparator implements BinaryPredicate{

HashMap weights;
IntComparator(HashMap f){
weights = f;
}
```

```
public boolean execute(Object first, Object second)
{
int firstVal =
    ((Integer)weights.get((Edge) first)).intValue();
int secondVal =
    ((Integer)weights.get((Edge) second)).intValue();
return firstVal < secondVal;
}


}
```

The interface `BinaryPredicate` requires the code for a Boolean method `execute` to be provided which defines the ordering. In the code above this ordering is based on the weights of each vertex.

The next lines of the Kruskal method are shown below:

```
Object u=null, v=null, distU, distV;
while(edgeList.size()!=0)
{
    Edge obtained = (Edge)edgeList.popFront();
    u = obtained.getFirst();
    v = obtained.getSecond();
    distU = ds.distinguished(u);
    distV = ds.distinguished(v);
    if(!distU.equals(distV))
    {
        a.add(obtained);
        ds.union(distU,distV);
    }
}
return a;
```

What this code does is to move along the linked list `edgeList` until it is exhausted, each time taking an element of the list from it which is an edge. If the two vertices associated with the edge are in the same set then it ignores them; however, if they are in different sets in the collection of disjoint sets then they are combined together to form a larger set and the edge added to the set a. When the processing of the linked list is completed a will contain the minimum spanning tree.

```
public HashSet Kruskal()
{
SList edgeList = new SList();
DisjointSet ds= new DisjointSet();
HashSet a = new HashSet();
Enumeration e = vertices.elements();
//Set up the collection of disjoint sets each
//containing one vertex
while(e.hasMoreElements()){
    Object vertex = e.nextElement();
    ds.add(vertex);
}
//Place all the edges on the edgeList
e = edges.elements();
while(e.hasMoreElements()){
    edgeList.pushBack(e.nextElement());
```

```
}
//Sort edgeList in decreasing order
Sorting.sort(edgeList, new IntComparator(weights));
Object u=null, v=null, distU, distV;
while(edgeList.size()!=0)
{
    //Take first (minimum edge) from the edge list
    Edge obtained = (Edge)edgeList.popFront();
    //Get the vertices associated with the edge
    u = obtained.getFirst();
    v = obtained.getSecond();
    //Get the distinguished elements: the sets which
    //contain the vertices in the edge
    distU = ds.distinguished(u);
    distV = ds.distinguished(v);
    if(!distU.equals(distV))
    {
        //The edges belong to separate sets so bring
        //them together using the union method
        a.add(obtained);
        ds.union(distU,distV);
    }
}
return a;
}
```

CHAPTER SUMMARY

▶ A graph implements relationships between a number of objects.

▶ A graph can be directed or undirected.

▶ A graph contains vertices and edges.

▶ A weighted graph has edges associated with some integer.

▶ There are a number of implementations of graphs ranging from simple but space-wasting implementations to those that are economical in space but require complex programming.

An Introduction to Patterns

This chapter:

▸ Motivates the need for patterns.
▸ Introduces three simple patterns: *Template, Decorator* and *Strategy*.

This chapter acts as an introduction to the remainder of the book—which is devoted to the subject of patterns.

11.1 Introduction

This book has progressed from looking in detail at data to the point where it has started looking at large-scale issues: class libraries and the development of larger and more complicated collections. This chapter proceeds further along this path by looking at patterns. These are commonly occurring collections of classes which promote reuse. In the following two chapters most of the patterns that are described will be focused around an application: that of a mailing list administration system. However, before looking at this system it is worth examining a number of small patterns[1].

11.2 The *Template* pattern

This section introduces a pattern known as *Template*. In order to introduce this pattern and the topic of patterns generally I will first present some

---

[1] Most of the patterns which are described in the next three chapters can be found *in Design Patterns*, E. Gamaa, R. Helm *et al*. Addison-Wesley, 1995.

code. The code is for an abstract class which specifies the interface to a collection of `Object` objects held in an array `holder`. The class implements common operations such as insertion and retrieval from a collection of objects.

11.2.1 The class `Collection`

The code for `Collection` is shown below:

```
abstract class Collection{

protected int        count;      //Count of items in array
protected int        size;       //Size of array
protected Object[]    holder;    //Array that holds objects

public Collection(int size)
{
//Sets up the collection with null values
count = 0;
holder = new Object [size];
for(int i = 0;i<size;i++)
   holder[i] = null;
this.size = size;
}

public Collection()
{
//Default constructor
this(100);
}


public void insertObject(Object o)
{
//Searches for o at an arbitrary position and
//steps over elements defined by nextPosition
//until an insertion point is found
int index=startInsertPosition(o);
count++;
while((holder[index]!=null))
   index = nextPosition(o,index);
holder[index]=o;
  }

public boolean findObject(Object o)
{
//Searches for o within the collection. Note
//that the objects contained in the collection must
//have equals defined for them
int index=startSearchPosition(o);
while((holder[index]!=null)&&!(holder[index].equals(o)))
   index = nextPosition(o,index);
return holder[index]!=null;
}
```

```
public void setCount(int count)
{
this.count = count;
}

public int getCount()
{
return count;
}

protected abstract int startSearchPosition(Object o);
protected abstract int startInsertPosition(Object o);
protected abstract int nextPosition(Object o,int index);

}
```

Before looking in detail at the class it is worth pointing out that it is abstract. This means that it contains abstract methods—in fact three of them. These abstract methods are not associated with any code; however, any class which inherits from `Collection` must provide code for these methods.

The instance variable `count` contains the number of items in the array and the instance variable `size` holds the size of the array `holder`. All the instance variables are protected so that subclasses can directly access them. There are a number of methods associated with this class, many of them are self explanatory so I shall focus in on the two methods `findObject` and `insertObject`

The method `findObject` returns true if the object that is its argument is found within the array `holder`. It carries out the process of finding the object by setting an index to some start position within the array and then steps over each element in the array looking for the object that is its argument. The way that the method moves to the next location in the array is defined by the method `nextPosition`. This method is abstract so the code for this is delegated to a subclass.

The method `findObject` employs two abstract methods `startSearchPosition` which sets the start position of the search and `nextPosition` which returns with an `int` that represents the next location of the array to search. These methods are abstract so that any subclass which implements `Collection` will need to define their code. This delegates it to the subclass to decide where to start the search and how to move from one element of the array to another element while carrying out the searching process.

The method `insertObject` inserts the object which is its argument into `holder`. It does this by examining a series of locations until an empty one is found; it then carries out the insertion. Again this method uses two abstract methods `startInsertPosition` and `nextPosition`. The method `startInsertPosition` determines which location in `holder` the start of the search for an empty location is to commence at. Again, since these methods are abstract, a subclass will determine the details of the search.

The class `Collection` is abstract and hence cannot be directly used. However, it provides much of the code required by its subclasses but delegates to its subclasses the specific search strategy to adopt.

SELF TEST QUESTION 1

Can you think of some specific strategies it could delegate?

11.2.2 Extending `Collection`

In order to see one particular strategy in action I shall present the code for a class `LinearCollection` which extends `Collection`. This class extends `Collection` and implements a linear search of `holder` starting at position 0 in the array; it is shown below:

```
public class LinearCollection extends Collection{

public LinearCollection(int size)
{
super(size);
}


public LinearCollection()
{
this(100);
}

public int startSearchPosition(Object o)
{
return 0;
}

public int startInsertPosition(Object o)
{
return count;
}

public int nextPosition(Object o, int index)
{
return ++index;
}

}
```

Here the position for starting a search is at the beginning of the array (0); the position for inserting an object into the array is just after the last object that has been added and the process of moving from one element of the array to the next is implemented via moving to the next sequential element. Notice that there is no error processing in the code; for example, when an item overflows the end of the array.

The code for `LinearCollection` implements the code for the abstract methods within `Collection`. It implements a simple, rather inefficient strategy of linear search. Let us now look at a more efficient implementation. This is shown below in the class `HashedCollection`.

It uses a hashing process. In this a hash function is used to determine where an object is going to be placed in an array. As you will remember from Chapter 4 this function should be carefully chosen so that most of the time it will generate the index of an empty location in `holder`, when it doesn't (a process known as a collision) a search is made from the insertion point until an empty location is found.

When an object is searched for, the hashing function is used to generate an initial search position; usually, this will immediately find the object being searched for; however, if it is not found then a new index is generated and the search starts from there. Normally hashing is a very fast process: if you choose a good hashing function then insertion and retrieval of objects is almost instantaneous.

The code for a class which extends `Collection` and uses hashing is shown below:

```
public  class HashedCollection extends Collection{

public HashedCollection (int size)
{
super(size);
}

public HashedCollection()
{
this(100);
}

public int startInsertPosition(Object o)
{
return calcPosition(o);
}

public int startSearchPosition(Object o)
{
return calcPosition(o);
}

public int nextPosition(Object o, int index)
{
return (index+index*index)%size;
}

private int calcPosition(Object o)
{
return o.hashCode()%size;
}
}
```

The important method within this class is `calcPosition`. This is a helper method which uses the method `hashCode` to generate a near unique `int` for the object which is its argument. In Java the built-in classes within the language all have `hashCode` defined for them and, so, if a `HashedCollection` object is to contain some built-in objects then nothing more needs to be done. If, however, you have defined your own classes which generate objects to be inserted into a `HashedCollection` object then you will need to write your own `hashCode` method for the classes.

The `hashCode` value that is generated within `calcPosition` is converted into an index for `holder` by dividing it by `size` (`size` represents the size of the array `holder` and is accessible from `HashedCollection` by virtue of the fact that it is protected) and taking the remaidner.

Both the methods `startPosition` and `insertPosition` will provide a starting position by using `calcPosition`. The collision of values is handled by a process known as quadratic resolution. In Chapter 4 we described collision resolution in terms of looking for the next unoccupied location. A more efficient process is to use a function containing a square term to determine which location is to be examined next. In the case of `HashedCollection` this is the function:

$$index + index^2$$

This, then, is discussion of the code that is an instantiation of a pattern known as *Template*. It is known as *Template* because the class `Collection` implements a template or skeleton for detailed code.

The *Template* pattern is effectively a reuse promoter: in the example above, much of the common code is embedded in the `Collection` class and all that a programmer needs to do to use the facilities of the class is to subclass it and provide code for the abstract methods.

It is worth pointing out that because the *Template* pattern provides a reuse advantage it suffers on another front: because it deals with generalities it has to define methods which are quite general where information is unused. For example, the method `nextPosition` has two arguments: an object defined by `Object` and an `int` which represents an index to `holder`. It specifies the object defined by `Object` to allow the programmer the option of calculating the next position for search or insertion based on the contents of the object.

Figure 11.1 shows a class diagram that describes the *Template* pattern. If a class is abstract then its name is italicised, if a method is abstract then it is preceded by the designator <>. Figure 11.1 also contains the graphical equivalent of a comment: a rectangular box with a corner folded down.

In Figure 11.1 the class `AbstractClass` (corresponding to `Collection`) contains two template methods: `templateMethod1` and `templateMethod2`, but it can contain more; in our examples these would be methods such as `insertObject`, `setCount` and `getCount` which would be concrete.

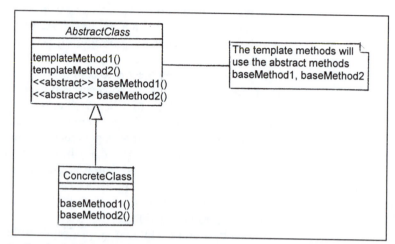

Figure 11.1 A
*class diagram
for the
Template
pattern*

It also includes two abstract methods `baseMethod1` and `baseMethod2` whose code is to be supplied by subclasses. In the case of our example, this would include methods such as `nextPosition` and `startInsertPosition`. The class `ConcreteClass` (corresponding to classes such as `LinearCollection`) then provides the concrete methods for those abstract methods in `AbstractClass`.

SELF TEST QUESTION 2

Write down the class diagram which is a concrete instantiation of Figure 11.1 for the collections that have previously been described.

The major point that you should notice about the *Template* pattern is that it provides a high degree of maintainability in a system: if you want to develop a `Collection` subclass which has a different set of algorithms for inserting or searching then all you need do is to provide the code for the methods `startInsertPosition`, `startSearchPosition` and `nextPosition`.

11.3 The *Strategy* pattern

The class diagram which describes the *Strategy* pattern is shown as Figure 11.2. The class `User` is comprised of a `Strategy` object, the line with the diamond indicating that such an object is an instance variable aggregated within `User`. The abstract class `Strategy` contains an abstract method `algorithm` which can vary within the subclasses of `Strategy`. The `User` class can gain values for the `Strategy` object either via a constructor or via a method which has a `Strategy` object as its argument. It is this object which determines what algorithm is going to be used by a `User` object. In Figure 11.2 only two concrete subclasses of `Strategy` are shown, many

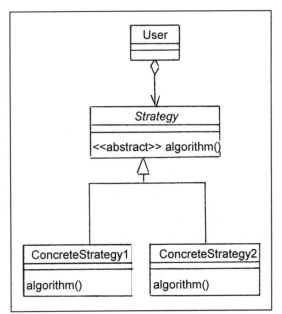

Figure 11.2
The Strategy
pattern

more are, of course, possible. A concrete example of this pattern is
described in the next section.

An example of the use of *Strategy*

A good example of the *Strategy* pattern can be demonstrated with an
extension of the `HashedCollection` class detailed in the previous section.
The code for this class is shown below:

```
public  class HashedCollection extends Collection
{

public HashedCollection (int size)
{
super(size);
}

public HashedCollection()
{
this(100);
}

public int startInsertPosition(Object o)
{
return calcPosition(o);
}

public int startSearchPosition(Object o)
{
return calcPosition(o);
}
```

```
public int nextPosition(Object o, int index)
{
return (index+index*index)%size;
}

private int calcPosition(Object o)
{
return o.hashCode()%size;
}

}
```

This class contains a method `nextPosition` which contains code for determining the next position to be examined if a collision occurs when inserting or finding an object in the `holder` array. In the code above this uses a quadratic function and is hardwired into the class; ideally we would like to vary the way in which `nextPosition` works. One way to get rid of the hardwired element of this class is via the *Strategy* pattern. In order to use this pattern we need an abstract class `NextPositionCalculator` shown below:

```
public abstract class NextPositionCalculator
{
public abstract int nextPosition(int val);
}
```

This class contains a single method which calculates the next position of the index to `holder` when a collision occurs. The `HashCollection` class now needs to be modified so that it contains a `NextPositionCalculator` object which can be used for the calculation. The code for the modified version of `HashedCollection` is shown below:

```
public class HashedCollection extends Collection{

private NextPositionCalculator hCalc;

public HashedCollection (int size, NextPositionCalculator
hCalc)
{
    super(size);
    this.hCalc = hCalc;
}

public HashedCollection(NextPositionCalculator hCalc)
{
    this(100, hCalc);
}

public int startInsertPosition(Object o)
{
    return calcPosition(o);
}

public int startSearchPosition(Object o)
{
    return calcPosition(o);
```

```
}

public int nextPosition(Object o, int index)
{
    return hCalc.nextPosition(index)%size;
}

private int calcPosition(Object o)
{
    return o.hashCode()%size;
}

}
```

Here, there is an instance variable hCalc which carries out the calculation. Its value is set by the constructors of the class. The code for nextPosition in hashedCollection then calculates the next position by sending the nextPosition message to the hCalc instance variable.

In order to set up HashedCollection objects with different collision strategies all that is needed is to implement a class which inherits from NextPositionCalculator and which overrides nextPosition with the code required to calculate the next index. For example, the class LinearNext, shown below, carries out the process of looking at the element in the array holder which is increment locations further on, where increment is an instance variable of LinearNext.

```
public class LinearNext extends NextPositionCalculator{

private int increment;

public LinearNext(int increment)
{
    this.increment = increment;
}

public int nextPosition(int index)
{
    return index+increment;
}

}
```

The code below

```
LinearNext ln = new LinearNext(20);
HashedCollection lc = new HashedCollection(100,ln);
```

sets up a HashedCollection object where the collision resolution algorithm involves moving on by 20 locations from the location where collision has occurred.

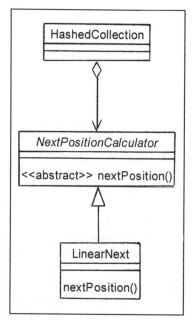

Figure 11.3 A concrete example of the Strategy pattern

This, then, is an example of the *Strategy* pattern; it is shown in Figure 11.3. The class HashedCollection corresponds to the class User in Figure 11.2; the class NextPositionCalculator corresponds to the class Strategy and the class LinearNext corresponds to one of the concrete strategy classes.

Both the *Template* and *Strategy* patterns now appear in the same chunk of software; the former is used to generate a family of algorithms, while the latter avoids hardwiring some of the details into one algorithm. Clearly in this case these two patterns are linked; this linking occurs time and time again in large systems. The combination of patterns and classes—both abstract and concrete—is known as a framework.

From the description of the patterns above you can see that they provide the user with flexible mechanisms for extending a system without changing very much code. For example, in the *Template* pattern example using the HashedCollection class a new strategy for determining the position for resolving collisions can easily be developed by communicating the strategy via a NextPositionCalculator object rather than by modifying the code of HashedCollection and recompiling.

11.4 The *Decorator* pattern

The *Decorator* pattern adds extra functionality to an object dynamically. Often the process of creating objects which have extra functionality is carried out by subclassing: extra methods are defined in a subclass of an existing class. However, in a number of cases this subclassing produces an explosion of subclasses and a very deep class hierarchy, where many

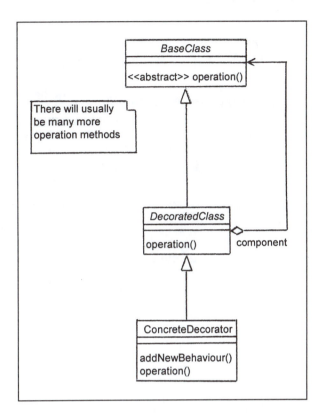

Figure 11.4
The Decorator
pattern

combinations of functionality have to be implemented. At the very least this leads to run-time inefficiencies and makes the class hierarchy difficult to manage.

The *Decorator* pattern allows classes to assume and drop responsibilities dynamically as a program is running. Figure 11.4 shows the general form of the *Decorator* pattern. The class BaseClass represents an abstract class which is extended to produce subclasses which will have responsibilities added or removed. The class defines a number of operations which have to be implemented in subclasses. One of these is operation. Figure 11.4 only shows one such method, in practice there may be a number; in the concrete example of this pattern described later in this section there are two.

The abstract class DecoratedClass is the superclass of all potential classes which have functionality dynamically added or removed. Figure 11.4 shows a concrete subclass ConcreteDecorator where extra functionality is added. In this concrete subclass the added functionality or behaviour is implemented via a method addNewBehavior. Within the class DecoratedClass there is an instance of BaseClass which is the destination object when the method operation is executed. Within the ConcreteDecorator class when operation is executed it results in the superclass method being executed followed by the additional functionality exemplified by addNewBehavior. This added behaviour can be parameterised so that it can change dynamically; for example, it could be encapsulated in an object which can be an instance variable of the class

ConcreteDecorator and which is set and unset by methods defined within this class; this is shown in the example below.

The example which I shall use to illustrate this pattern is connected with the development of PrintWriter objects which can transform the strings they process. In Java the PrintWriter class is used to write character data to a stream including strings. The example presented here develops a class which has this responsibility, but also is capable of transforming the strings which are to be displayed. In order to do this a class is needed which extends the existing PrintWriter class. This is shown below

```
public   class ExtendedPrintWriter extends  PrintWriter{

private PrintWriter component;

public ExtendedPrintWriter(PrintWriter pw)
{
super(pw);
component = pw;
}

public void print(String s)
{
component.print(s);
}

public void println(String s)
{
component.println(s);
}

}
```

This class corresponds to the class DecoratedClass in Figure 11.4, the only difference here is that PrintWriter is a concrete class. In extending PrintWriter it holds an instance variable component which is used within the methods print and println that override the corresponding methods in PrintWriter. The code for these two methods just apply the methods to the PrintWriter object component. Thus, the methods print and println correspond to the operation method in Figure 11.4. The class corresponding to ConcreteDecorator in Figure 11.4 is shown below:

```
public class TransformerExtendedPrintWriter extends
                ExtendedPrintWriter {

Transformer cs;

public TransformerExtendedPrintWriter
        (PrintWriter pw, Transformer c)
{
    super(pw);
    cs = c;
}
```

```
public void resetTransformer(Transformer c)
{
    cs = c;
}

public void print(String s)
{
    String  transformed = cs.transform(s);
    super.print(transformed);
}

public void println(String s)
{
    String  transformed = cs.transform(s);
    super.println(transformed);
}

}
```

The class uses an object defined by `Transformer` which carries out the process of transforming the string to be printed using the `PrintWriter` class. The method `transform` within this class contains the code that carries out the transformation.

The code within this class is relatively straightforward: the constructor just constructs an object defined by the class by employing the superclass constructor and initialises the `Transformer` object which is to carry out the transformation. The method `resetTransformer` allows the user of objects defined by the class to dynamically add responsibilities to the class, replacing the transformation algorithm with a new one during the execution of a system containing `TransformerExtendedPrintWriter` objects. The two methods `print` and `println` are similar, they correspond to `operation` in Figure 11.4 and first apply the new behaviour and then call their corresponding methods in the superclass, in this way the transformation is carried out before the printing.

Given the class `TransformerExtendedPrintWriter` we can now define a whole number of objects which print strings after some transformation has occurred, with the transformation being anything we wish to define by means of subclassing the class `Transformer`.

SELF TEST QUESTION 3

Write down the code which creates a `TransformerExtendedPrintWriter` object which writes to `System.out`, autoflushes and applies a transformation to two adjacent characters so that they are compressed to a single character. Assume the class which defines this transformation is `TwoCharCompressor`.

The code which is the answer to the above self test question is shown below:

```
TransformerExtendedPrintWriter cepw =
```

```
new TransformerExtendedPrintWriter
    (new PrintWriter(System.out,true),new
                              TwoCharCompressor());
```

This creates an object which is based on a `PrintWriter` that writes to the `System.out` stream and autoflushes (the role of the true valued second argument) and to which the functionality in a `TwoCharCompressor` object is applied. This object, which is based on a class which subclasses `Transformer`, carries out a simple compression of the text by replacing frequent pairs of characters with a single character resulting in a compressed text.

The `cepw` object detailed in the solution to the self test question can then have its responsibility dynamically changed by the code

```
cepw.resetTransformer(new ThreeCharCompressor());
```

which sets the `Transformer` object to be an object which carries out text compression based on replacing common three-character sequences with a single character. Again, the `ThreeCharCompressor` class is a subclass of `Transformer`.

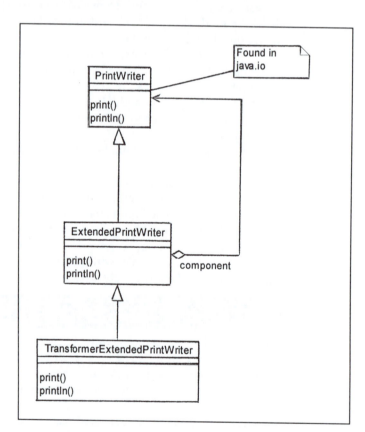

Figure 11.5 A concrete instantiation of the Decorator pattern

New `TransformerExtendedPrintWriter` objects can easily be set up which carry out a variety of transformations. For example the code

```
TransformerExtendedPrintWriter cepw =
    new TransformerExtendedPrintWriter
            (new PrintWriter(System.out,true),
                new asteriskTerminator());
```

where `asteriskTerminator` is a subclass of `Transformer` whose objects carry out the process of adding a terminating asterisk to the string which is to be printed.

What is worth noticing is the fact that my description of the concrete instaniation of the *Decorator* pattern contains an example of the *Strategy* pattern: the `Transformer` object allows different strategies for printing to be communicated to the `TransformerExtendedPrintWriter` class.

Figure 11.5 shows the instantiation of the *Decorator* pattern for the transformation example described above.

CHAPTER SUMMARY

▶ A pattern is a collection of classes which is replicated over a number of applications.

▶ Patterns normally rely on the use of abstract classes.

▶ Patterns make use of inheritance and aggregation.

The *Composite* Pattern

This chapter:

▸ Introduces the *Composite* pattern.
▸ Describes the use of the *Composite* pattern in a real context.
▸ Outlines other uses for the *Composite* pattern.

The previous chapter looked at some small patterns in relative isolation. This chapter looks at a real application and how one pattern is used in it.

12.1 An application

The application which will be used to illustrate some further patterns is that of a mailing list administration system. Electronic mailing lists are groups of users who have been registered with the administration system as recipients of electronic mail messages which are of interest to them. For example, in a software company there may be a mailing list for marketing staff which provides them with up-to-date news on products.

Such a system requires a number of mailing lists to be maintained; each list will contain groups of users who have informed the administration program that they wish to receive electronic mail which is directed to a specific group. In the rest of the book I shall refer to a group of users who belong to a particular mailing list as *user groups*. Figure 12.1 shows the organisation of users and user groups within a mailing list administration program. The organisation of the mailing list is shown as a hierarchy, with the oval entities representing groups and the rectangles representing individuals who have registered with a particular group. In Figure 12.1 only a small part of the hierarchy is shown; for example, the

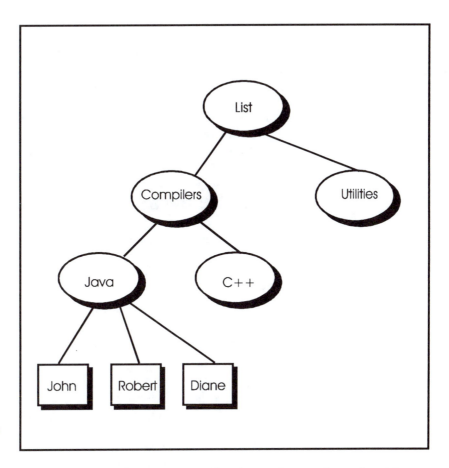

**Figure 12.1
The
organisation
of mailing lists**

group interested in C++ compilers is not shown. The oval entities are known as composites, while the rectangles are known as leaves.

What distinguishes a leaf from a composite is the fact that a composite can contain a number of further leaves or composites, while a leaf is a terminator. This arrangement allows users to register their interest for a general topic such as compilers or for a more specific topic such as C++ compilers that are marketed by Microsoft.

An important point to make about the arrangement of groups and users is that a group is functionally very similar to a user: for example, an email can be sent to both entities. This point lies at the heart of the composite pattern and is what gives it its power.

The administrator functions are exercised by the human administrator of the system. These functions will include:

▶ setting up new user groups;

▶ deleting existing user groups;

▶ adding a new user to a group;

▶ removing a user from a group;

▶ querying the collection of user groups and users for information such as the members of a particular group.

These functions are instigated by the human administrator invoking a program which displays a frame that contains menu items, text fields and list boxes which provide the concrete means of exercising the functions. This frame is shown in Figure 12.2. Here the menus provide facilities such as deleting users, deleting user groups, finding all the users associated with a group, finding all the groups and querying the groups or users using some search string.

12.2 The data

Groups of users (composites) and users (leaves) are functionally very similar in that they are both emailable. How can this fact be used to develop code for part of the email administration system? Consider the abstract class `Mailable` shown below:

```
public abstract class Mailable{

String name;

public abstract void mail();
public abstract void removeAll();
public abstract void addMailable(Mailable m)
            throws KnownMailableException;
public abstract void removeMailable(Mailable m)
            throws UnknownMailableException;
public abstract Mailable findMailable(String name);
public abstract Enumeration getChildren();
public abstract void setName(String name);
public abstract String getName();
}
```

The methods for this class are:

▶ `mail`. This carries out the process of sending an email to a mailable object, this will either be an individual user or groups of users.

▶ `removeAll`. This removes all the children of a mailable object and the object itself if the object is a user group; if it a single user then it just removes the object.

▶ `addMailable`. This adds a mailable object to a user group. The method generates an exception if the object to be added already exists.

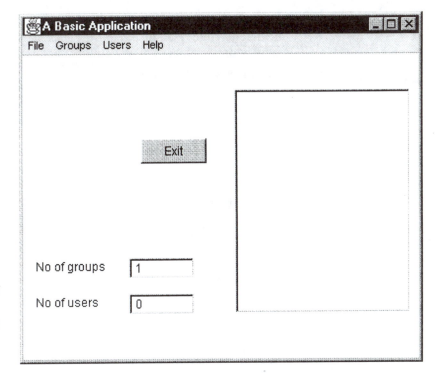

Figure 12.2 A screen shot of the administration window

▶ `removeMailable`. This removes a mailable object from a user group. The method generates an exception if the object to be removed does not exist in the group.

▶ `findMailable`. This finds a mailable object which lies under its argument in the hierarchy of mailing groups and users.

▶ `getChildren`. This returns an enumeration of all the children in a user group.

▶ `setName`. This sets the name of a mailable object. The name uniquely identifies the object. For a user group this will be the name of the group; for a user this will be the name of the user.

▶ `getName`. This returns with the name of a mailable object.

This class can be used as a superclass to those classes which can be used to represent users or user groups. Two examples of such classes are shown below: one represents users and the other represents groups.

12.3 The class `UserGroup`

The first class is `UserGroup` which represents a group of users. The class has an instance variable defined by the class `Children` below. This class is based on the JGL `HashMap` class which implements a key/value data

structure that allows rapid reading and writing. It is used to implement
the parent–child relationship in the *Composite* pattern: it holds
name/address values of all the children associated with a `Mailable` object.

```
public class Children extends HashMap{

Children()
{
   super();
}


}
```

The code for the `UserGroup` class is:

```
public class UserGroup extends Mailable{

Children holder;

public UserGroup()
{
//Gives the top node of the composite the name "Root"
this("Root");
}

public UserGroup(String name)
{
//Constructor for a user group
this.name = name;
holder = new Children();
noOfChildren = 0;
}

public void removeMailable(Mailable m)
      throws UnknownMailableException
{
String name = m.getName();
Enumeration e;
Mailable target = (Mailable)holder.get(name);
if(target == null)
   throw new UnknownMailableException();
else
{
   //Get the children who form part of the group
   e = getChildren();
   while (e.hasMoreElements())
   {
      //Move over the children deleting all
      //their children if they exist. This
      //method uses the removeAll method below
      String s = (String)e.nextElement();
      Mailable nm = (Mailable) holder.get(s);
      if(s.equals(nm.getName()))
         nm.removeAll();
   }
   //Remove the parent
```

```
        holder.remove(m.getName());
    }
}

public void removeAll()
{
Enumeration e = holder.elements();
//Recursively remove all the children
//and their children etc.
while(e.hasMoreElements())
{
    Mailable nm = (Mailable)e.nextElement();
    nm.removeAll();
}
}

public void mail()
{
//Code for mail, not shown
}


public void addMailable(Mailable m)throws
                  KnownMailableException
{
String s = m.getName();
Mailable ms = (Mailable)holder.get(s);
if(!(ms == null))
    throw new KnownMailableException();
else
    //place an association between the
    //name of the mailing list and
    //the mailable entity in the HashMap.
    //This could be a user or
    //another group
    holder.put(s, m);
}

public void setName(String name)
{
this.name = name;
}

public String getName()
{
return name;
}

public Enumeration getChildren()
{
return holder.keys();
}

public Mailable findMailable(String name)
{
Enumeration e;
```

```
Mailable m, n;
//Have we found the mailable?
if (this.getName().equals(name))
   return this;
else
   {
       //Wander over the children looking
       //for the mailable object
       e = holder.keys();
       while(e.hasMoreElements())
       {
          String s = (String)e.nextElement();
          m = (Mailable) holder.get(s);
          //Recursive search down each child
          n = m.findMailable(name);
          if(!(n == null))
             return n;
       }
   }
return null;
}


}
```

Much of the code is self-explanatory. I have omitted the code for mailing since it is implementation specific. The method `removeMailable` has as its target a `Mailable` object and has as an argument the `Mailable` object which is to be deleted. The search for the latter argument starts at the destination object which acts as a root point. Once the object to be deleted has been found the method `removeAll` is executed, this removes both the object to be deleted and all its children.

The method `addMailable` just adds a new child to an existing mailable object by adding a key/value pair to the `holder` instance variable which implements the parent/child relationship.

A very important point to make about the code above is that is deals with `Mailable` objects, this means that any object which inherits from `Mailable` can be inserted into a mailing list. In the next section we shall see individual users described by a class which inherits from `Mailable`. However, other `Mailable` classes can be defined; for example, high security mailing lists. The pattern that is unfolding allows us to easily extend our mailing list.

12.4 The class `User`

The second class is `User`. It describes objects which are single users who are members of groups. The class represents objects which are leaves; hence, a number of the inherited methods are not defined since they try to add, remove and access children of the leaf. In order to overcome this problem each of these methods throws an exception. The code for the class is shown below; it inherits from `Mailable`.

```
public  class User extends Mailable{
```

```
EmailAddress address;
int          instanceCount;

public User(EmailAddress address, String name)
{
this.address = address;
this.name = name;
instanceCount = 1;
}

public Enumeration getChildren() throws ChildException
{
throw new ChildException
   ("Attempt to access children from a single user");
}

public void removeMailable(Mailable m) throws ChildException
{
throw new ChildException
   ("Attempt to remove a child from a single user");
}

public void removeAll()
{
//Uses the method delete found in UserFactory
UserFactory uf = UserFactory.getInstanceOfUserFactory();
uf.deleteUser(address);
}

public void mail()
{
//Code for mailing
}

public Enumeration elements() throws ChildException
{
throw new ChildException
   ("Attempt to get a child from a single user");
}

public void addMailable(Mailable m)
{
throw new ChildException
   ("Attempt to add a child to a single user");
}

public void setUserName(String name)
{
this.name = name;
}

public String getUserName()
{
return name;
}
```

```
public void setName(String address)
{
this.address = new EmailAddress(address);
}

public String getName()
{
return address.getAddress();
}

public Mailable findMailable(String name){
if((this.name).equals(name))
    return this;
else
    return null;
}

public void setInstanceCount(int val)
{
instanceCount = val;
}

public int getInstanceCount()
{
return instanceCount;
}


}
```

It is worth briefly describing how each of these classes handle the operation of mailing. The method `mail` in the class `User` would include code that would interact with the current mailing utility which the administration program was configured for[1].

The method `mail` in the class `UserGroup` would iterate through `children` sending the message `mail` to each of the objects contained in the array. If the object in the array was a `UserGroup` object then it would use mail recursively; however, if it was a `User` object then `mail` in the class `User` would be used.

The `User` class has three instance variables. The first is the name of the user inherited from `Mailable`, the second is the email address of the user. There is also a third instance variable which keeps track of the number of times each user is contained in the objects which implement the composite pattern, the role of this variable is discussed in the next chapter.

The class also contains a number of methods which are inherited from `Mailable`, but which are not really defined for a user. These methods are associated with operations on the children of an emailable object. In the code for `User` these generate a `ChildException` object.

---

[1] This would of course mean that the program would be non-portable. For example, if it had to interact with the MAPI mailing software in Windows 95/98 then something like Visual J++ would be used to generate the code and it would be impossible to move it to another platform directly.

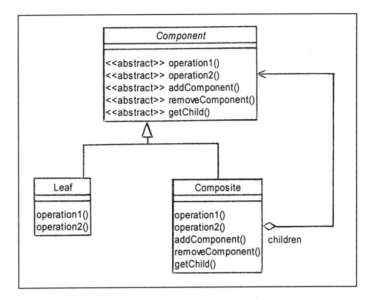

***Figure 12.3 The
general form of
the Composite
pattern***

The method `removeAll` which, in the case of a `UserGroup`, removes a
parent and all its children, just removes the user. To do this it makes use
of a static method `deleteUser` from the class `UserFactory`. The details of
this class are shown in the next chapter. `deleteUser` effectively deletes a
user from the collection of users which are in existence.

The only other method worth mentioning is `findMailable`. In the case
of the class `UserGroup` this starts a search for a mailable object from the
destination object in the tree which implemented the *Composite* pattern,
and either returns `null` if the object was not found or returns the object
itself if it was found. All `findMailable` does in the class `User` is to
examine the `User` object to check that it is the one that is being searched
for; if it is, then it returns the object, if it isn't, then `null` is returned.

This, then, is an example of a useful pattern. The code skeleton for this
pattern is shown below and its class diagram is shown in Figure 12.3. This
only shows two operations, there can be many more.

```
abstract class Component{

public abstract returnType1 operation1(argument list)
public abstract returnType2 operation2(argument list)
..
public abstract returnTypen operationn(argument list)
public abstract void addComponent(Component c)
public abstract void removeComponent(Component c)
public abstract Component getChild(int i);
}
```

The methods starting with `operation` correspond to operations on
individual elements of the composite; `addComponent` adds a component to

a part of the tree; `removeComponent` removes a component and `getChild` returns with the *i*th child of a composite.

This abstract class embodies the essence of the *Composite* pattern: it allows the development of leaves and composites and also allows the development of code which maintains and accesses a tree structure made up of these elements. Such a tree structure occurs time and time again in computer systems. For example, it occurs in:

▶ Manufacturing applications in which products are manipulated, where a product consists of subproducts (composites) and components (leaves). For example, in a car manufacturing system a car might consist of composites such as an engine and leaves such as a gearshift lever. In this case a typical operation, which would be the analogue of `mail`, would be one which calculated the cost of an individual subproduct or component.

▶ Drawing applications, where the objects involved could be simple shapes such as squares (leaves) or collections of objects (composites). A typical operation would be one which moved a drawing object in some direction.

▶ Operating systems where users (leaves) are split into user groups (composites). A typical operation would be one which assigned a certain security level to either a user or a whole group of users.

All these applications will contain classes that can be generated from the *Composite* pattern, the only difference between them being the operation that is applied to composites and leaves. In the case of the mailing list administration program the operation would involve mailing to groups or users; in the case of the manufacturing application it could be an operation to calculate the cost of a composite or leaf or calculate the amount of wiring required if the product is a piece of electrical equipment.

Figure 12.3 describes the *Composite* pattern graphically. Here the class `Component` corresponds to the class `Mailable` and the class `Composite` corresponds to the class `UserGroup`. The class `Leaf` corresponds to the class `User`. The operations `operation1`, `operation2` etc. correspond to methods such as `mail`, `setUserName` and `getUserName`. Figure 12.4 shows the instantiation of the pattern for the email system.

It is worth pointing out at this stage that *Composite* has a number of variants. For example, instead of declaring the methods `addComponent` and `removeComponent` in the abstract class `Component` we could have removed them and just implemented them without extending the composite subclass.

SELF TEST QUESTION 1

What would be the advantages and disadvantages of instead of declaring the methods `addComponent` and `removeComponent` in the abstract class

`Component` removing them and just implementing them without extending the composite subclass?

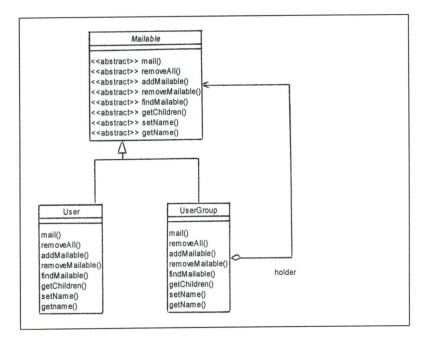

Figure 12.4
The
instantiation
of the
Composite
pattern within
the email
system

The important point implied by the answer to the previous self test question is that all patterns exhibit variants and that, almost invariably, these variants involve trade-offs between qualities such as transparency and the ability to monitor some errors at compile time (safety).

CHAPTER SUMMARY

▶ Patterns are given a name which can be used in talking to other designers and in cataloguing.

▶ Patterns solve a problem. The pattern *Composite* solved the problem of providing uniform access to an object which consists of leaf objects and composites that contain other objects.

▶ Patterns provide a solution. This solution is expressed in terms of abstract classes and interfaces, not in terms of concrete code. Although I did use concrete code to show how the patterns work out in practice the essence of a pattern is often expressed in classes which cannot be directly used to instantiate objects.

▶ They embody decisions about trade-offs. The normal trade-offs are between space, execution time and programming complexity. An example of a simple trade-off was that shown in the *Composite* pattern where child management methods were embedded in the high-level class `UserGroup` rather than the next level composite class.

CHAPTER 13

Patterns and the Mailing List Application

CHAPTER OVERVIEW

This chapter:

▶ Describes the *Visitor* pattern.
▶ Describes the *Builder* pattern.
▶ Shows how the *Builder* pattern and the *Visitor* pattern can be combined.
▶ Describes the *Flyweight* pattern.

This is the final chapter and looks at the use of three patterns in the mailing list system described previously.

13.1 Introduction

There is often a need for a class which contains a collection and which allows easy access to the objects in it on an object-by-object basis. For example, in a manufacturing application where products are made up from other products and components (a product which cannot be split up any further) there would be a need for the following operations:

▶ An operation which would traverse the data structure holding the product and calculating the overall material cost of the product. Each of the items in the collection would be visited and a cost accumulated.

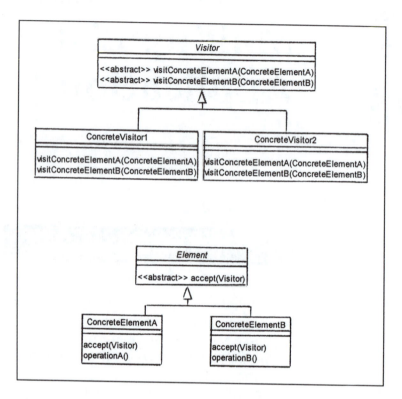

Figure 13.1 The Visitor pattern

▶ An operation which would traverse the data structure holding a product and accumulating the number and type of components in order to decide whether there was enough stock available to produce a production run of a particular product.

▶ An operation which would traverse the data structure holding a product in order to determine which components in the product could be substituted for cheaper components.

The *Visitor* pattern enables functionality associated with traversing a collection of objects to be implemented without modifying the class which describes the collection. Effectively it allows the developer to develop code which implements functionality without altering the basic class structure of the collection class.

It does this by embedding a method `accept` within the class describing elements of the collection (`Element`). The method `accept` takes an argument which is an object from another class which implements the visiting functionality. The class diagram for this is shown in Figure 13.1[1].

In this figure the class `Visitor` defines objects which visit the collection of objects to be processed. This abstract class will contain methods which implement the functionality associated with a visit. The

---

[1] As with the vast majority of patterns presented in this and the previous chapter *Visitor* is based on those found in E. Gamma, R. Helm *et al*, *Design Patterns*, Addison-Wesley, 1995.

methods are given the name `visitConcreteElementA` and
`visitConcreteElementB` within `Visitor`.

The abstract class `Element` defines the individual elements of a
structure which is to be visited. The subclasses of this class will contain a
method `accept` which carries out the element-by-element processing. The
type of processing that is to occur will depend on the class of the argument
to `accept` since it has a `visitConcreteElement` method within its
argument which is executed by `accept`. This is an example of a technique
known as a callback. The use of a callback means that you can pass
different objects to `accept` which have different functionality associated
with them without altering the code within `Element`.

13.2 The *Visitor* pattern and the email list administration program

One of the functions of the administrator part of the email list
administration system described in the previous chapter is to produce a
listing of the groups that are being administered and also a listing of the
members of each group. Initially the specification of the system asked for
an HTML listing, with groups being represented by their name and a
hyperlink to their group listing. The listing below shows an example of the
typical HTML source generated:

```
<HTML>
<HEAD>
<TITLE> Compilers</TITLE></HEAD>
<BODY>
<H2> Listing of group <I> Compilers </I></H2>
<TABLE>
<TR>
<TD>GROUP </TD>
<TD><I> COBOLCompilers</I></TD>
<TD> Click here ---- &gt; </TD>
<TD>
<A HREF="COBOLCompilers.htm">COBOLCompilers</A>
</TD></TR>
<TR>
<TD>GROUP </TD>
<TD><I> CCompilers</I></TD>
<TD> Click here ---- &gt; </TD>
<TD>
<A HREF="CCompilers.htm">CCompilers</A>
</TD></TR>
<TR>
<TD>GROUP </TD>
<TD><I> FORTRANCompilers</I></TD>
<TD> Click here ---- &gt; </TD>
<TD>
<A HREF="FORTRANCompilers.htm">FORTRANCompilers</A>
</TD></TR>
<TR>
<TD>USER </TD>
```

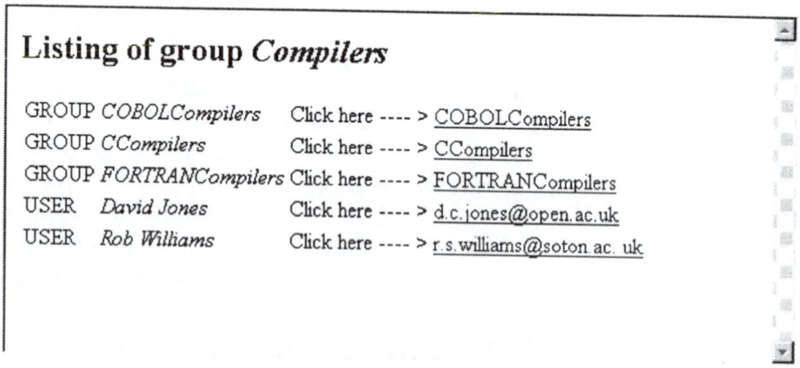

**Figure 13.2
The display
of a user
group within
Internet
Explorer**

Listing of group *Compilers*

GROUP	*COBOLCompilers*	Click here ---- >	COBOLCompilers
GROUP	*CCompilers*	Click here ---- >	CCompilers
GROUP	*FORTRANCompilers*	Click here ---- >	FORTRANCompilers
USER	*David Jones*	Click here ---- >	d.c.jones@open.ac.uk
USER	*Rob Williams*	Click here ---- >	r.s.williams@soton.ac. uk

```
<TD><I> David Jones </I></TD>
<TD> Click here ---- &gt;</TD>
<TD><A HREF="mailto:d.c.jones@open.ac.uk">
d.c.jones@open.ac.uk</A>
</TD></TR>
<TR>
<TD>USER </TD>
<TD><I> Rob Williams </I></TD>
<TD> Click here ---- &gt;</TD>
<TD><A
HREF="mailto:r.s.williams@soton.ac.uk">r.s.williams@soton.ac
. uk</A>
</TD></TR></TABLE></BODY></HTML>
```

Figure 13.2 shows the display of this HTML file within a browser. The specification requires the development of an overall listing of the groups with hyperlinks to each group and a listing of members for each group. If the member of the group is a user then the name of the user is displayed together with their email address; if the member is a further group then the name of the group is listed in such a way that the user of a browser is able to click on it and move to the member listing of the group. When listing users the email identity should be displayed in such a way that a browser user can click on it and the native mailing system is executed in order to send an email to that user.

This functionality is ripe for an implementation via the *Visitor* pattern: the processing that occurs is that of writing text in an HTML format to the various files which contain the listing of groups and the listing of users and subgroups.

13.2.1 The implementation

The first part of the implementation is the code for the abstract class `MailableVisitor`. This corresponds to the class `Visitor` in Figure 13.1. You will remember from Chapter 12 that a `Mailable` object is one to which email messages can be sent: in this application these will be users and user groups.

13.2.2 The abstract class

The abstract class `MailableVisitor` is shown below:

```
public abstract class MailableVisitor
{
    public abstract void visitUser(Mailable m);
    public abstract void visitUserGroup(Mailable m);
    public abstract void leaveUserGroup(Mailable m);
}
```

The three abstract methods within `MailableVisitor` correspond to the `visit` methods within `Visitor`. The method `visitUser` carries out the functionality of visiting an individual user: in the case of the listing functions it will produce some HTML code which displays the name of the user and his or her email address.

The method `visitUserGroup` will carry out the functionality of displaying the details of a user group and the method `leaveUserGroup`, which is invoked when processing moves to another user group, will set up a new HTML file for the new group being visited.

The code for `HTMLPrintingVisitor` is next presented. This is the concrete subclass of `MailableVisitor` which carries out the writing of HTML code to the files used for listing both user groups and users. In this class methods such as `visitUser` and `VisitUserGroup` correspond to methods such as `visitConcreteElementA` in Figure 13.1. These are the methods which do the work when visiting an element of the composite which holds mailing list details. Two files are created: the first which is attached to the `PrintStream` object `po` is the file which will hold details of the current user group being processed; the second attached to `summaryStream` is a file which will contain details of all the user groups.

13.2.3 The concrete visitors

```
public class HTMLPrintingVisitor extends MailableVisitor{

private PrintStream po;      //Current PrintStream

private Stack st;            //Stack used for storing past
                             //streams

private PrintStream summaryStream; //The stream used for the
                                   //list of user groups

private String directoryChosen;    //The name of the
                                   //directory that the user
                                   //has chosen

public HTMLPrintingVisitor
        (String nameOfNode, PrintStream summaryStream,
```

```
              String directoryChosen)
{
try
{
   //Set up a new HTML file
   po = new PrintStream (new FileOutputStream
         (directoryChosen+nameOfNode+".htm"));
   st = new Stack();
   //Place the file on the stack
   st.push(po);
   this.summaryStream = summaryStream;
   this.directoryChosen = directoryChosen;
}
catch(IOException e)
   {System.out.println("Problem setting up print stream");};
}


public void visitUser(Mailable item)
{
po = (PrintStream)st.peek();
User userId = (User)item;
String userName = userId.getUserName(),
emailAddress = item.getName();
//Writes the user name and the user's email address
//Into a row of a table using <TR> and <TD>
po.println("<TR><TD> USER <TD><I>"+userName +
         "</I><TD> Click here----><TD>"+
         "<A HREF = \"mailto:"+emailAddress+"\">"+
         emailAddress+"</A>"+"\n");
}


public void visitUserGroup(Mailable item)
{
try
{
   po = (PrintStream)st.peek();
   String groupName = item.getName();
   //Writes the name of the group to the
   //summary listing of groups using the HTML tags
   //<TR> and <TD> which define a row of a table
   summaryStream.println
     ("<TR><TD>GROUP <TD><I>"+groupName+
      "</I><TD>Click here----> <TD> "+
      "<A HREF=\""+groupName+".htm\">"+groupName+"</A>");
   //Writes the group name as a hyperlink to
   //the current file being processed
   po.println
     ("<TR><TD>GROUP <TD><I>"+groupName+
      "</I><TD>Click here----> <TD> "+
      "<A HREF=\""+groupName+".htm\">"+groupName+"</A>");
   //We have now stopped processing the
   //current user group and need to set
   //up a new file containing the members
   //of that group.The current Printstream
```

```
          //needs to be placed on the stack since there
          //may be further members to process when
          //we return from the lower level groups.
          po = new PrintStream(new
               FileOutputStream(directoryChosen+item.getName()+
                                  ".htm"));
          st.push(po);
          //Writes an HTML header to the file together
          //with the header of an HTML table. We are
          //using HTML tables to display users and user groups
          po.println
             ("<HTML><HEAD><TITLE>"+
              groupName+"</TITLE></HEAD><BODY>"+"\n");
          po.println
             ("<H2> Listing of group <I>"+ groupName +
              "</I></H2>"+"\n");
          po.println("<TABLE>");
     }
catch(IOException e)
   {System.out.println("Problem setting up print stream");}
   }

public void leaveUserGroup(Mailable item)
{
String groupName = item.getName();
//Get the current PrintStream at the top of
//the stack without destroying it
po = (PrintStream)st.peek();
//Write the end of the HTMl file
po.println("</TABLE>");
po.println("</BODY></HTML>");
po.close();
st.pop();
}


}
```

There are a number of details which need a little explanation. First, the class has a stack (first-in last-out) `st` as an instance variable. This is used to store `PrintStream` objects. Each HTML file which contains the details of a user group will be stored in a separate file which is given the name of the user group followed by '.htm'. When we are in the middle of processing the members of a group, and the current object we are processing is another user group, then we will need to set up a file for that new group and write the members of the new group to the file which has the name of the group. However, we will need to return to our original file when we return to processing the remaining members of the group that was exited from. In order to store the `PrintStream` so that it can be later retrieved we use a `Stack` object and push the `PrintStream` onto the stack when we move down to deal with a new group.

The second detail is that the class has an instance variable `directoryChosen` which has been specified by the user; all the HTML files that are produced are placed in this directory.

The class also has a `PrintStream` instance variable `summaryStream` which is used to connect to the file containing the list of user groups. The code for the methods is fairly straightforward. The only processing that needs explanation is the detailed HTML that is written.

The method `visitUser` will write lines such as

```
<TR><TD> USER <TD><I>David Jones</I><TD> Click here----><TD
<A HREF = "mailto:D.Jones@Libenrat.com"> emailAddress</A>
```

The tag `<TR>` defines a line in an HTML table, the tag `<TD>` introduces an element of the table, the tag `<A>` introduces a clickable link and the tag `<I>` italicises the text it references; in the case of the code above this link is an email reference which initiates the native email system so that the user of the browser can send email messages to the designated user.

The method `visitUserGroup` will display the user group details on the current `PrintStream` object, lines such as

```
<TR><TD>GROUP <TD><I>+groupName</I><TD>Click here----> <TD>
<A HREF= "JavaCompilers.htm" JavaCompilers</A>"
```

will be generated. Here the `<A>` tag is used to generate a clickable link which takes the user of a browser to the user group which is referenced. The method also generates a similar line which is written to the `PrintStream` object attached to the file containing a list of all the user groups. The method `visitUserGroup` also writes header text to the new file which has been generated containing the members of the group which is currently being processed. This will look like

```
<HTML><HEAD><TITLE>JavaCompilers</TITLE>
</HEAD><BODY>
<H2> Listing of group <I>JavaCompilers</I>
</H2>
<TABLE>
```

The first two lines identify the HTML file, the third and fourth line writes its name in a large font and the final line sets up the table in which the users and user groups are to be displayed.

The method `leaveUserGroup` is invoked when the processing reaches the end of a user group i.e., when there are no more groups or users left to process. It writes a footer to the HTML file

```
</TABLE>
</BODY></HTML>
```

and then pops the last `PrintStream` object used from the stack so that processing can resume at the point within the last file that was generated before carrying out the current processing.

13.2.4 Visiting the `Mailable` objects

The remaining code to be described belongs to the `Mailable` objects in the email list administration system. In the mail system the class `Mailable` corresponds to `Element` within Figure 13.1. In order for listing to occur there is a need for `accept` methods within `User` and `UserGroup` classes described in Chapter 12; these correspond to the `accept` methods within the concrete subclasses `ConcreteElementA` and `ConcreteElementB`.

The first method is `accept` within `UserGroup`:

```
public void accept(MailableVisitor hv)
{
Enumeration children = getChildren();
Mailable m=null;
String nm;
hv.visitUserGroup(this);
while(children.hasMoreElements())
{
    nm = (String)children.nextElement();
    m = findMailable(nm);
    m.accept(hv);
}
hv.leaveUserGroup(this);
}
```

What this does is to traverse the objects which make up the *Composite* pattern instance and apply the `visitUserGroup` method to the element to generate the HTML code for the group; it then applies `accept` recursively so that its children are then processed; the children can of course be either user groups or users. When the method has returned from processing the children the final processing in `leaveUserGroup` is applied and the HTML code that finishes the current file is written.

The next method is `accept` within `User`. This is very simple:

```
public  void accept(MailableVisitor hv)
{
hv.visitUser(this);
}
```

All it does is to use `visitUser` which writes HTML code which describes a user.

13.2.5 Executing the listing function

The only remaining code interrogates the user for the directory that is required and carries out the generation of the HTML files. This is shown below:

```
public void execute()
{
try
{
    String directoryChosen = null;
    FileDialog fd =
                new FileDialog(parentFrame,
                "Choice of summary file",FileDialog.SAVE);
    fd.setVisible(true);
    String fileChosenName = fd.getFile();
    directoryChosen = fd.getDirectory();
```

```
                //Set up the file containing a
                //list of user groups

                PrintStream summaryPrintst =
                        new PrintStream
                        (new FileOutputStream(directoryChosen
                                +fileChosenName+".htm"));
                summaryPrintst.println
                        ("<HTML><HEAD><TITLE>" + " Summary of groups"+
                        "</TITLE></HEAD><BODY>"+"\n");
                summaryPrintst.println
                        ("<H2> Listing of all
                        groups"+"</H2>"+"\n");
                summaryPrintst.println
                                ("<TABLE>");
                //Start the visiting process, root contains
                //the Mailable object at the top of the Composite
                root.accept(
                    new HTMLPrintingVisitor(root.getName(),summaryPrintst,
                                        directoryChosen));
                //Write terminating lines to the summary file
                summaryPrintst.println("</TABLE>");
                summaryPrintst.println("</BODY></HTML>");
                summaryPrintst.close();
        }
        catch(Exception i)
            {System.out.println
                    ("Problem setting up summary file");}
        }
```

All this does is to find out into which directory the user wishes to place the HTML files, set up the summary file which will contain the collection of groups and start the visiting process. It terminates after writing footer information to the summary file.

Given these classes, adding functionality to the mailing list administration program is easy and would not require any further changes to the User and UserGroup classes. For example, consider a change which asked for the details of the groups to be displayed in a format to be specified by the user—such as SGML[2], RTF[3] or LaTeX[4]. All that would be required is for classes to be developed which would be subclasses of MailableVisitor, each corresponding to a document format.

The code for the methods visitUser, visitUserGroup and leaveUserGroup would then need to be developed and would just involve programming println statements which issued the relevant elements of the document formatting language. There is, however, another more flexible solution; it involves a pattern known as *Builder*.

---

[2] SGML is a popular document processing markup language on which HTML was based.
[3] RTF stands for rich text format. This is the internal character form that Microsoft uses to store Word documents. Current plans by Microsoft envisage downplaying this format with respect to HTML.
[4] LaTeX is a popular typesetting language used by mathematicians.

13.3 The *Builder* pattern

The *Builder* pattern is shown in Figure 13.3. There are two main classes that are involved in this pattern. First, there is UserOfBuilder, which is the class that uses classes derived from the Builder class to produce some object. The *Builder* class is an abstract class from which a number of subclasses are derived. Each of these classes correspond to a different representation of an object that is to be built up. The UserOfBuilder class has an aggregation relationship with an object which is described by Builder.

The class Builder contains a number of methods which construct and add components to the object being built up. These are shown as buildPart1 to buildPartn. So, for example, if the object to be built up was a table then the class Builder might contain methods which generate the heading of the table, each row of the table and the final footer of the table.

The concrete subclasses of Builder represent different representations of the objects to be built up. In our example the object to be built up is the text which describes the mailing lists. In the previous section this text was generated as HTML so that it could be displayed using a Web browser. However, in the future we might want some other textual formatting language to be used; for example, the next few years should see a growth in the markup language XML[5].

The code for the ReportBuilder class which is used in the email list system is shown below, it corresponds to Builder in Figure 13.3:

```
public abstract class ReportBuilder
{
public abstract void header(PrintStream ps);
public abstract void userDetails
    PrintStream ps, String user, String address);
public abstract void terminator(PrintStream ps);
public abstract void
    groupHeader(PrintStream ps, String groupName);
public abstract void
    groupDetails(PrintStream summaryStream, PrintStream ps,
                 String groupName);
}
```

The method header will produce a header for the document to be constructed; userDetails produces the details of each user of the email system; terminator will produce the final text for the report; groupHeader will produce the heading of each mailing list group and groupDetails will display the details of each group.

The class HTMLBuilder which produces an HTML listing is shown below; this corresponds to one of the concrete subclasses of Builder:

---

[5] XML is a largish subset of the SGML document processing language on which HTML was based. It overcomes many of the problems in HTML in that it is relatively easy to define extensions to the language.

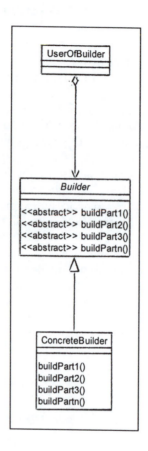

**Figure 13.3
The Builder
pattern**

```
public class HTMLBuilder extends ReportBuilder{

public  void header(PrintStream ps)
{
ps.println
   ("<HTML><HEAD><TITLE>" + " Summary of
   groups"+"</TITLE></HEAD><BODY>"+"\n");
ps.println
   ("<H2> Listing of all groups "+"</H2>"+"\n");
ps.println
   ("<TABLE>");
}

public  void userDetails
    (PrintStream ps, String name, String address)
{
ps.println("<TR><TD> USER <TD><I>"+name +
        "</I><TD> Click here----><TD>"+
        "<A HREF = \"mailto:"+address+"\">"+
                address+"</A>"+"\n");
}

public  void terminator(PrintStream ps)
```

```
{
ps.println("</TABLE>");
ps.println("</BODY></HTML>");
ps.close();
}


public  void groupHeader(PrintStream ps, String groupName)
{
ps.println
    ("<HTML><HEAD><TITLE>" +
     groupName+"</TITLE></HEAD><BODY>"+"\n");
ps.println
    ("<H2> Listing of group<I>"+groupName+
     "</I></H2>"+"\n");
ps.println
    ("<TABLE>");
}


public  void groupDetails
    (PrintStream summaryStream, PrintStream ps,
     String groupName)
{
summaryStream.println
    ("<TR><TD>GROUP <TD><I>"+groupName+
     "</I><TD>Click here----> <TD> "
     +"<A HREF=\""+groupName+".htm\">"+
     groupName+"</A>");
//Writes the group name as a hyperlink to the current
//file being processed
ps.println
    ("<TR><TD>GROUP <TD><I>"+groupName+
     "</I><TD>Click here----> <TD> "+
     "<A HREF=\""+groupName+".htm\">"+groupName+"</A>");
}


}
```

Objects of the type ReportBuilder could then be used within a class
described by the *Visitor* pattern. They would be communicated to the class
as an argument to its constructors. Code in the methods of the
MailableVisitor class, instead of having the HTML generation
hardwired into them, would just send messages corresponding to
groupDetails and terminator to the Builder object that forms part of
the MailableVisitor class. If a change in specification was required to
change the format to another one, say XML, then all that would be needed
would be for a new ReportBuilder subclass to be constructed whose
methods would generate XML statements. An object defined by this class
would then again be communicated to the MailableVisitor class by
means of a constructor and the required code generated.

13.4 The *Flyweight* pattern

13.4.1 Introduction

In the book which introduced patterns to the computing community[6] the *Flyweight* pattern is introduced by showing its relevance in the design of a document processing system. In such a system objects representing characters are stored in a document. Each object is associated with its state: data which is solely connected with that object. In the document processing system this would be data associated with that particular instance: the font that the character is associated with, its size, its style (normal, bold, italic) and its value. This is shown in Figure 13.4 where a small part of a document consisting of the words 'The cat' are shown together with the state of the character *T*.

In this example there could potentially be a large number of characters; if these were all implemented in terms of objects in a simple-minded way then there would be major problems with storage. However, the *Flyweight* pattern provides an alternative. With this pattern each character is implemented once, and a pointer to each unique character object is embedded in the text. If you count capital letters and lower case letters as distinct this would mean that there would only be a requirement for about a 100 character objects. However, there is a problem: a large amount of data is associated with each character which will be different for each instance of the character in the document. For example, each character in a document would be associated with a font and a size.

The solution to this problem is to develop a data structure which provides details about this part of the character state in such a way that the space involved is minimised. One way to do this is shown in Figure 13.5. Here a data structure keeps track of where each component of the state changes. For example, assume that the document was initially written using the Times Roman font, then there would be a marker which said that the first character is in this font.

Now, suppose that at character 44 the font changed to Courier, the data structure would then record this change and if it changed back to Times Roman at character 60 then, again, this data would be included in the data structure.

Figure 13.5 represents that part of the data structure which describes font changes. Similar collections of data describe changes to font size and style. Because such changes occur infrequently such data structures will not consume large amounts of memory.

This example allows me to define two components of an object which are important in understanding the *Flyweight* pattern. The first is the extrinsic state of an object. This is that data which will change from each instance of an object; in the document example this includes the name of the font and the size of the font.

---

[6] E. Gamma, R. Helm *et al*, *Design Patterns*, Addison-Wesley, 1995.

Figure 13.4
Part of a
document

The second is the intrinsic state of an object. This is that part of the state which is common across all potential instances of an object and thus has the capability of being stored only once; for example, the internal code and glyph of the character.

13.4.2 Users and the Flyweight pattern

The users of the mailing system provide us with an example where we could use the *Flyweight* pattern. Each user will be associated with an email address and a name. There will also be user data about which groups the user is registered with. Another potential set of data will also be associated with the fact that users may be registered with the system as having particular mailing problems.

The problem would be indicated by emails which have been sent to the user but which have been bounced back with some message that the user is unable to be mailed. This could happen for a number of reasons: the user may no longer exist, he or she could have left the organisation to which the email has been sent or there could be some temporary problem with the user's network. Dealing with such users can be tricky. One solution is to arrange for the system to delete the user as soon as a bounced email is encountered.

This is a drastic solution. Another solution is to keep some historical data about the bounces; for example, when they occurred, whether there were any intermediate successful emails etc. If the latter strategy was adopted, then each user will have quite a large data structure contained in its state.

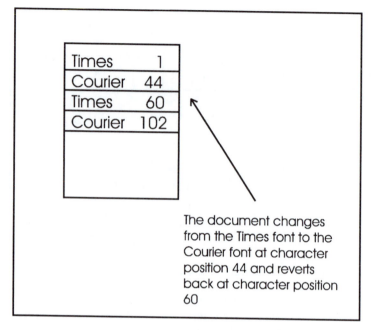

Figure 13.5 Part of a data structure describing a document

The document changes from the Times font to the Courier font at character position 44 and reverts back at character position 60

If we assume that there are a large number of users who will be registered with a number of mail groups then there could be a potential for memory problems. In order to solve this problem we use the *Flyweight* pattern. In using this pattern I shall assume the following:

▶ That the intrinsic state is the name of the user and the data structure which holds bounce information.

▶ That the extrinsic state is the collection of separate groups that the user is associated with. By *separate* I mean those groups which are not sub-groups of other groups in the state.

▶ That each user is identified by a key and that he or she is represented by the email address of the user.

The general form of the *Flyweight* pattern is shown below. Figure 13.6 shows the graphical version.

```
public class FlyweightFactory{

//Instance variable which relates a key to a single
//instance of a Flyweight object

Public Flyweight getFlyweight(Key val)
{
//Code for returning a Flyweight object
```

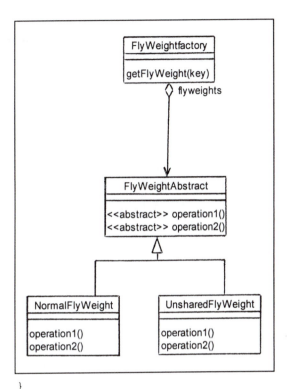

**Figure 13.6
the Flyweight
pattern**

```
}

}

public abstract class FlyweightAbstract
{
//Abstract method headers for a number of operations
//which are applied to Flyweight objects
}

class NormalFlyweight extends Flyweight
{
//Code for the abstract methods defined in Flyweight
}

class UnsharedFlyweight extends Flyweight
{
//Code for the abstract methods defined in Flyweight
}
```

The class `FlyweightFactory` contains one method `getFlyweight`. What this method does is to read the key which is its argument and searches the data structure instance variable which keeps track of the `Flyweight` objects that have been created. If the `Flyweight` object is found then it is returned; if not, it is created, added to the data structure and then returned.

The abstract `FlyweightAbstract` class specifies the objects which are possibly to be shared. Two concrete classes `NormalFlyweight` and

UnsharedFlyweight inherit from Flyweight, these are used to implement the objects which are to be manipulated; the former implements objects which are to be shared, while the latter implements unshared objects if they were required in the application. In the document example which was used for the initial motivation in this chapter, the class NormalFlyweight would implement shared character data, while the class UnsharedFlyweight would implement unshared character data.

In the mailing administration program the users will be implemented as Flyweight objects defined by the class User. I shall assume that they will all be shared. The reflection of the *Flyweight* pattern in the class UserFactory is shown below:

```
public class UserFactory{

//factory associates a key with the user
//The key is the email address

protected  HashMap factory = null;
private static UserFactory instance = null;

private UserFactory()
{
factory = new HashMap();
}

public static UserFactory getInstanceOfUserFactory()
{
if (instance ==null)
{
   //UserFactory has not yet been created
   instance = new UserFactory();
}
return instance;
}

public User createUser(EmailAddress em, String name)
{
User u;
User foundUser = (User)factory.get(em.getAddress());
if (foundUser == null)
{
   //User has not been created, create one
   factory.put
      (em.getAddress(), u =new User(em, name));
   return u;
}
else
{
   //User has been created, add one to the instance count
   int count = foundUser.getInstanceCount();
   count++;
   foundUser.setInstanceCount(count);
   factory.put(em.getAddress(), foundUser);
   return foundUser;
}
```

```
}

public  User findUser(EmailAddress em)
{
User foundUser = (User) factory.get(em.getAddress());
return foundUser;
}

public  void deleteUser(EmailAddress em){
User foundUser = (User)factory.get(em.getAddress());
int count = foundUser.getInstanceCount();
count--;
if(count==0)
    //No instances of the user
    factory.remove(em.getAddress());
else
    //There are still further instances, so write back
    //the user with the decremented count back to factory
    factory.put(em.getAddress(),foundUser);
}
}
```

The class uses the JGL HashMap object factory which associates each
flyweight with its key; in the case of users this will be the email address.
Each user is associated with a count which will contain the number of
occurrences of that user within the data structure holding the membership
of mailing lists since a user may be registered with any number of lists. In
Chapter 12 you will remember that the class User was associated with an
instanceCount instance variable. The method getInstanceCount in
User returns the current value of this variable.

The createUser method creates a user. If that user already exists (he
or she will already be registered as a member of an existing email list)
then all that happens is that the user details are retrieved and the count of
the number of occurrences of that user incremented: if the user does not
exist then he or she is created with the User constructor setting the count
of occurrences to one. The deleteUser method will retrieve details about
the user and then decrement the count of the number of occurrences of
that user within the mailing lists. If the count is then zero this means that
the user does not occur within the mailing list and he or she is completely
deleted from the HashMap containing the users.

CHAPTER SUMMARY

▶ The *Visitor* pattern allows a collection of objects to be traversed in order to
apply some operation to individual objects in the collection.

▶ The *Builder* pattern allow data structures to be built up in such a way
that their construction is decoupled from their representation.

▶ The *Flyweight* pattern enables common data to be shared.

Appendix

This appendix contains the solutions to all the self test questions posed in the book.

Chapter 1

Self Test Question 1

There are a number of operations. A selection is shown below:

▸ An operation which adds a new user to the group of users.

▸ An operation which adds an email to the collection of emails associated with a specific user.

▸ An operation which adds a user to a particular group.

▸ An operation which removes a user from a group.

▸ An operation which deletes all the emails corresponding to the members of a specific group and them moves all the group to another group.

▸ An operation which moves a user from one group to another.

Self Test Question 2

There could be a number of primitive operations. A selection is shown below:

▸ An operation which first checks that the group exists.

▸ An operation which retrieves the members of the group.

▸ An operation which deletes an email associated with a member of the group.

▶ An operation which takes a member of a group and adds him or her to another group.

▶ An operation which deletes a group.

Self Test Question 3

A map since it is used to relate one collection of data (the computers) to another collection of data (the traffic conditions).

Self Test Question 4

There are a number:

▶ The addition of a computer to the network.

▶ The addition of linking information between a computer and other computers in the network.

▶ The removal of a computer from the network.

▶ The removal of linking data for a computer in a network.

▶ The modification of routing data for a computer; for example, when a new computer is added which connects to another computer.

There are many others, this is just a selection.

Chapter 2

Self Test Question 1

There are at least three further operations:

▶ An operation which initialises the queue of blocks waiting to be used for files. This operation will be invoked when the operating system is started up.

▶ An operation which returns a collection of blocks to the collection of free blocks waiting to be used for files. The collection will be taken from the queue of blocks waiting to be returned.

▶ An operation which checks whether there is enough space in the collection of blocks to satisfy the creation of a file.

Self Test Question 2

There are a number of operations:

▶ An operation which checks that a particular user is stored in an instance of the data type.

▶ An operation which removes a user from an instance of the data type.

▶ An operation which takes a user identity and then returns with the password associated with the user.

▶ An operation which returns with the number of users stored in an instance of the data type.

▶ An operation which changes the password associated with a particular user.

Self Test Question 3

There are a number of operations:

▶ The operation which checks that a particular user is stored in an instance of the data type would correspond to the action that occurs when a user logs on to the operating system.

▶ The operation which removes a user from an instance of the data type occurs whenever the system administrator wants to removes a user, for example, when that user leaves.

▶ The operation which takes a user identity and then returns with the password associated with the user would correspond to the system administrator finding out the password of a user when, for example, the user had forgotten the password.

▶ The operation which returns with the number of users stored in an instance of the data type might be invoked when the system administrator wanted to find out how many current users the operating system is supporting.

▶ The operation which changes the password associated with a particular user would be associated with the user changing his or her password, perhaps when the maximum time allowed for the password expires.

Self Test Question 4

Some of the operations are shown below:

▶ An operation which adds an order to the queue.

▶ An operation which removes the first order from the queue.

▶ An operation which deletes an order from the middle of the queue.

Self Test Question 5

Some of the operations are shown below:

▶ An operation which checks whether the queue is empty.

▶ An operation which discovers whether a particular order is in the queue.

▶ An operation which checks whether there are any duplicate orders in the queue.

▶ An operation which counts the number of items in the queue.

Self Test Question 6

The first two examples are both sets: they consist of a collection of unique items. The third and fourth examples are not strictly sets since they consist of two collections of data which are associated with each other. They are maps.

Self Test Question 7

The first and third collections would employ sets; the second collection would employ a sequence, items in such a sequence would normally be added in the order in which they arrive at a computer.

Self Test Question 8

The first data type would be a set and the second a sequence. The third and fourth would be maps. In the third the map would be associated with the set of employees and the set of cars, while the fourth would be a map associated with the set of lorries and the set of destinations.

Self Test Question 9

The first would be a map which mapped rooms to the set of employees in each room; the second would be a set; the third would be a graph and the fourth would be a map from customers to some indication of business volume.

Chapter 3

Self Test Question 1

The code is shown below. The exception classes are not shown.

```
public class SimpleIntSetException{

private int        maxSize,   //Maximum size of the set
                   count;     //Count of the elements in set
private int[]      holder;    //Array used to implement set

SimpleIntSetException(int maxSize)
{
this.maxSize = maxSize;
count =0;
holder = new int[maxSize+1];
}

SimpleIntSetException()
{
this(50);
}

public void add(int val)
        throws SetFullException, DuplicateElementException
{
if(findIndex(val)!=count)
    throw new DuplicateElementException();
if (count == maxSize)
    throw new SetFullException();
holder[count] = val;
count++;
}

public void remove(int val)
        throws ElementNotFoundException
{
int index = findIndex(val);
if(index==count)
    throw new ElementNotFoundException();
//Copy elements after found element
for(int k = index;k<count-1;k++)
    holder[k]=holder[k+1];
count--;
}

public int count()
{
return count;
}

public int maxSize()
{
return maxSize;
}

public boolean isIn(int val)
{
int foundIndex = findIndex(val);
return foundIndex<count;
}
```

```
private int findIndex(int val)
{
//Uses sentinel at position count
int k =0;
holder[count] = val;
while(holder[k]!= val)
    k++;
return k;
}

}
```

Self Test Question 2

First, is it memory efficient? Yes, it is almost optimal in terms of memory: only one extra memory location is used over and above those used for storing integers. Is it efficient in terms of run-time? The answer again is yes, for searching the method isIn runs in a time proportional to $\log_2(n)$ (where again, n is the size of the array) since the algorithm iteratively cuts the array in half each time that it looks for the integer to be found. The methods for removing and adding integers involve a linear process in which elements are examined one-by-one. This process is proportional to n. These methods could be programmed to make them more efficient by carrying out a binary search for the integer nearest to or equal to the integer to be added or removed.

In terms of programming, the complexity of this implementation is higher. It involves some tricky looping in findIndex and add, with the potential of errors being made in programming the stopping point. So this implementation has gained speed and has traded this off in programming complexity terms. This is a common story in the implementation of abstract data types: a gain in one area results in a loss in another.

Self Test Question 3

The code is shown below:

```
public class RangeBooleanIntSet
{

private int     count,          //Count of elements in set
                maxSize,        //Maximum size of set
                upper,          //Upper value limit
                lower;          //Lower value limit

private boolean[]    holder;            //Array implementing set

RangeBooleanIntSet(int lower, int upper)
{
count = 0;
holder = new boolean[upper-lower+1];
```

```
for(int j = 0;j<upper-lower+1;j++)
    holder[j] = false;
maxSize = upper-lower+1;
this.lower = lower;
this.upper = upper;
}

public void add(int val)
        throws OutOfRangeException, DuplicateElementException
{
if(val<lower||val>upper)
    throw new OutOfRangeException();
if (holder[val-lower])
    throw new DuplicateElementException();
holder[val-lower] = true;
count++;
}

public void remove(int val)
        throws ElementNotFoundException,OutOfRangeException
{
if(val<lower||val>upper)
    throw new OutOfRangeException();
if (!holder[val-lower])
    throw new ElementNotFoundException();
holder[val-lower] = false;
count--;
}

public int count()
{
return count;
}

public int maxSize()
{
return maxSize;
}

public boolean isIn(int val)
{
return holder[val-lower];
}

}
```

Chapter 4

Self Test Question 1

This is the simplest implementation that I could have chosen. The programming is minimal and relies on an existing collection class. It uses a small amount of memory but suffers from performance problems: the contains method within the Vector class searches in a linear fashion.

Self Test Question 2

It is more complex in terms of programming complexity. Many of the operations are faster except for add which, because the vector is ordered, needs to be searched for an insertion point. It uses the same amount of memory as the previous implementation.

Self Test Question 3

The code is shown below:

```
class OrderedPair implements CompObject{

private Integer     first,
                    second;

OrderedPair(int first, int second)
{
this.first = new Integer(first);
this.second = new Integer(second);
}

public int compareTo(Object o)
{
int a = first.intValue(),
    b = second.intValue();
int c = (((OrderedPair)o).first).intValue(),
    d = (((OrderedPair)o).second).intValue();
if(a>c)
   return 1;
else
   if(a<c)
      return -1;
   else
      if (b>d)
         return 1;
      else
         return -1;
}

}
```

Self Test Question 4

The code is shown below:

```
private int findIndex(Vector v, Object o, int cap)
{
//Hash value calculated by dividing the hash code
//by the capacity of the vector.
```

```
//Returns the index to the found location of o or the
//first null location that has been encountered
int hCode = o.hashCode();
//hashCode can return zero or negative values
//from built in classes such as String!!
if (hCode<0)
    hCode-=hCode;
int index = hCode%cap;
//Loop around looking for o or first null entry
while((v.elementAt(index)!=null))
{
    if((v.elementAt(index)).equals(o))
        break;
    if (index == cap-1)
        index = 0;
    else
        index++;
}
return index;
}
```

Self Test Question 5

You can say that it is very poor: a good hashing function should map values uniformly within the vector. The four elements in the vector should be spread evenly, not bunched up.

Self Test Question 6

The code is shown below:

```
public void add(Object o)
{
//Find the hash value
int index = findIndex(o,holder.capacity());
Vector v = (Vector)holder.elementAt(index);
v.addElement(o);
holder.setElementAt(v,index);
count++;
}

public void remove(Object o)
{
//Find the hash value
int index = findIndex(o,holder.capacity());
Vector v = (Vector)holder.elementAt(index);
//Remove the object o from the Vector at this index
v.removeElement(o);
holder.setElementAt(v,index);
count--;
}
```

Self Test Question 7

The code is shown below:

```
public CompObject findMinimum() throws EmptySetException
{
if(count()==0)
    throw new EmptySetException();
TreeNode temp = pointer;
//Move down every left pointer until null is encountered
while(temp.getLeft()!=null)
    temp=temp.getLeft();
return temp.getData();
}
```

Self Test Question 8

The code is shown below:

```
public Enumeration elementsDecreasing()
{
Vector contents = new Vector();
collectDecreasing(contents,pointer);
return contents.elements();
}


private void collectDecreasing(Vector v, TreeNode p)
{
if(p.getRight()!=null)
    collectDecreasing(v,p.getRight());
v.addElement(p.getData());
if(p.getLeft()!= null)
    collectDecreasing(v,p.getLeft());
}
```

Chapter 5

Self Test Question 1

The code is shown below:

```
public boolean isKeyIn(Object key)
{
    return holder.containsKey(key);
}
```

Self Test Question 2

The code is shown below:

```
public void deleteItem(Object key, Object item)
          throws KeyMissingException, ItemMissingException
{
if(!holder.containsKey(key))
   //No key corresponding to key
   throw new KeyMissingException();
Vector v = (Vector)holder.get(key);
if(!v.contains(item))
     //Item to be deleted from vector is not found
     throw new ItemMissingException();
v.removeElement(item);
holder.put(key,v);
}
```

Self Test Question 3

The code is shown below. It retrieves the Vector object associated with the key and then uses the Vector method elements to return the Enumeration object associated with it.

```
public Enumeration itemElements(Object key)throws
KeyMissingException
{
if(!holder.containsKey(key))
   //Unknown key
   throw new KeyMissingException();
Vector v = (Vector)holder.get(key);
return v.elements();
}
```

Self Test Question 4

The code is shown below:

```
public int getBalance(String accHolder, String accountName)
      throws NoAccountException, NoAccountHolderException,
             NumberFormatException
{
String accts = assoc.getProperty(accHolder,"NotFound");
//Account holder not found
if(accts.equals("NotFound"))
   throw new NoAccountHolderException();
String val = findAccountValue(accountName,accHolder);
if(val.equals(""))
   //Account not found
   throw new NoAccountException()
return Integer.parseInt(val);
}
```

This method uses the helper method `findAccountValue` which returns the balance of an account as a string. This is converted into an `int` by the static method `parseInt` which throws a `NumberFormatException` object if the string which is its argument is not a valid number

Chapter 6

Self Test Question 1

The code is shown below:

```
public void push(Object o)
{
    holder.insertElementAt(o, count);
    count++;
}

public Object pop()throws EmptyStackException
{
    if(holder.size() == 0)
        //The stack is empty
        throw new EmptyStackException();
    count--;
    return holder.elementAt(count);
}
```

Self Test Question 2

The code is shown below:

```
public void add(Object o)
{
back=increment(back);
holder[back] = o;
count++;
}

public Object remove()
{
Object frontValue = holder[front];
front = increment(front);
count--;
return frontValue;
}
```

This code is relatively straightforward, all it does is to either deposit an object at the end of the queue for `add` or remove an object from the front of the queue for `remove`. It makes use of `increment` to handle the housekeeping of the index.

Self Test Question 3

The code is shown below:

```
class FixedQueueEnumerator implements Enumeration{

int        arraySize,   //Size of the array
           index,       //Current index
           count,       //Count of the elements in the queue
           counter;     //Counts elements in the queue
Object[]   holder;      //Holds elements in the queue

FixedQueueEnumerator
      (Object[] holder, int arraySize, int front, int count)
{
this.arraySize = arraySize;
this.count = count;
index = front;
this.holder=holder;
counter=0;
}

public boolean hasMoreElements()
{
//From Enumeration
return count != counter;
}

public Object nextElement()
{
//From Enumeration
Object temp = holder[index];
counter++;
if(index == (arraySize-1))
   //End of queue
   index = 0;
else
   //Space to increment
   index++;
return temp;
}

}
```

Self Test Question 4

The main disadvantage is that it is a fixed-size implementation. In order to use the queue you need to estimate the maximum size of the queue. If this maximum size is not attained then there will be wasted space in the queue during its lifetime. The solution is to include code in add which increments the queue by a specified amount when it becomes full. This increment can be communicated to the class via its constructor. There are much better solutions to this problem, and one which involves dynamic memory allocation is detailed in the next subsection.

Self Test Question 5

The code is shown below:

```
public void add(Object o)
{
if(count==0)
    head = tail = new ElementPointer(o);
else
{
    //Adjust last element to point at new element o
    ElementPointer temp = new ElementPointer(o);
    tail.setNext(temp);
    tail = temp;
}
count++;
}
```

If there are no elements in the queue it creates a single element and points `head` and `tail` at it; if not, it creates a new element and points `tail` at it. Finally, it increments the count of elements.

Self Test Question 6

The code is shown below:

```
public boolean inQueue(Object o)
{
ElementPointer traverser = head;
boolean found = false;
while(traverser != null)
{
    if((traverser.getData()).equals(o))
    {
        found = true; //Element has been found
        break;          //Exit the loop
    }
traverser = traverser.getNext();
}
return found;
}
```

It repeatedly loops down the queue looking for the element to find; when it finds it the loop is exited.

Self Test Question 7

The code is shown below:

```
public void remove(CompObject o)
{
ElementPointer  traverser = header.getNext(),
                           previous = header;
//Move over sequence looking for element
while(((CompObject)traverser.getData()).compareTo(o)!=0)
{
   previous = traverser;
   traverser = traverser.getNext();
}
//Found it, adjust pointers to delete it
previous.setNext(traverser.getNext());
count--;
}
```

This repeatedly travels down the queue looking for the element to be
removed. When it finds it, it adjusts the pointer of the preceding element
to point at the element following the one to be deleted. Remember that
compareTo will deliver a zero int if its destination object and argument
are equal.

Self Test Question 8

The code is shown below:

```
public boolean isIn(CompObject o)
{
ElementPointer traverser = header.getNext();
//Traverse sequence until either sentinel
//is found or o is encountered
while((traverser != header) &&
((CompObject)traverser.getData()).compareTo(o)!=0)
    traverser = traverser.getNext();
return traverser != header;
}
```

This repeatedly travels down the queue looking for the element to be
found. It terminates the search either when the end of the sequence is
encountered or the element that is being searched for is found.

Self Test Question 9

The code is shown below:

```
public void remove(CompObject o)
{
ElementTwoPointer traverser = header.getNext();
while(((CompObject)traverser.getData()).compareTo(o)!=0)
    traverser = traverser.getNext();
ElementTwoPointer before = traverser.getPrevious(),
                  after = traverser.getNext();
```

```
before.setNext(after);
after.setPrevious(before);
count--;
}
```

This is similar to add: all it does is to loop until it finds the deletion point and then adjusts the pointers of the elements after and before the element to be deleted so that the element no longer plays a part in the sequence. Again, since a doubly linked list is employed, there is no need to keep continual track of the previous element in the list using a local variable.

Self Test Question 10

No, it also allows the list to be processed in two directions: forward and back. For example, you could define a method which delivered an Enumeration object which allowed the list to be accessed from its end rather than from its beginning.

Chapter 7

Self Test Question 1

There would be many different entities involved, a selection is shown below:

▶ The collection of user names.

▶ Instance variables which related the user to the various allowances they were allocated; for example, the maximum amount of file space that they were allowed to use.

▶ Details of any privileges that they were given; for example, whether they were allowed to access certain areas of the file store.

▶ Details of where the users are located; for example, which departments they can be found in.

Self Test Question 2

▶ If the operating system contained reusable components from other existing operating systems, then this would be an example of aggregation.

▶ This would be an example of aggregation

▶ This would be an example of composition.

Self Test Question 3

The first change is to extend the class `IntegerSet` so as to form a new class called, say, `EfficientSet` which will contain the instance variable `sum`. Next, since the sum needs to be updated when an integer is added to the set we need to override the `insert` method. Also, since the `findSum` method will return with the instance variable value then this would need to be overriden.

Self Test Question 4

The answer really depends on the occupancy of the `Hashtable`. If it was heavily loaded and required a number of searches to locate an object then yes, it would be an effective use. However, if the loading was light, say less than 60%, then most retrievals would only involve processing one element in the `HashTable` and hence there would be less need for the two instance variables.

Self Test Question 5

Any collection where lookup will take time and where a particular object is to be frequently looked up would benefit from the device. For example, sequences are normally searched linearly; the use of an extra object would make a substantial difference.

Self Test Question 6

If you look at the code for `EfficientSet` which was derived from inheriting from `IntegerSet` then you will see that it is shorter and simpler; however, it will prove to be less efficient. It does have the advantage that if there was a change in functionality in `IntegerSet`—such as the addition of a new method—then that method would automatically be available in `EfficentSet` provided, of course, that it did not affect the instance variable `sum`. In the case where composition is used effort would need to be expended by the programmer since the code for the set would need to be modified and re-tested—a much greater effort than in the inheritance case. There is a further point to make about inheritance which is concerned with changes to the methods in a class which is a superclass to a number of other classes. If the signature of a method (the number and types of its arguments and return type) changes in that class then all the code that uses this class will need to be changed.

Chapter 9

Self Test Question 1

The code is shown below:

```
public void setVal(int row, int column, Object o)
   throws RowException, ColumnException
{
if (row > maxRow)
   throw new RowException();
if(column > maxColumn)
   throw new ColumnException();
array.put(new RowColumn(row,column), o);
}
```

Self Test Question 2

The code is shown below:

```
public void registerUser(EmailUser eu)throws
IllegalArgumentException{
Object o = subscribers.add(eu);
if(o!=null)
    throw new IllegalArgumentException("User already
registered");
}
```

Self Test Question 3

The code is shown below:

```
public void removeFromGroup(EmailUser eu, String gp)
                   throws IllegalArgumentException
{
if (groups.count(gp)!=1)
   throw new IllegalArgumentException
       ("Group does not exist");
//User must already be registered
if (subscribers.count(eu)!=1)
   throw new IllegalArgumentException
         ("User not registered");
HashSet val = (HashSet)groups.get(gp);
if(val.count(eu)==0)
   throw new IllegalArgumentException
             ("User not registered with group");
val.remove(eu);
groups.put(gp,val);
}
```

Self Test Question 4

The code is shown below:

```
public HashSet allInBoth(String gp1, String gp2)throws
                                      IllegalArgumentException
{
if (groups.count(gp1)!=1)
   throw new IllegalArgumentException
          ("Group does not exist");
if (groups.count(gp2)!=1)
      throw new IllegalArgumentException
          ("Group does not exist");
HashSet hs1 = (HashSet)groups.get(gp1);
HashSet hs2 = (HashSet)groups.get(gp2);
return hs1.union(hs2);
}
```

Self Test Question 5

It would need a `HashMap` object which mapped words onto the documents which contained them. These documents would be stored as a set of some sort.

Chapter 10

Self Test Question 1

This implementation suffers from two problems: first it is limited to graphs whose elements are integers which range from 1 to some upper limit; second, it is somewhat wasteful of space. In mitigation it must be said that it is a very simple implementation to program.

Self Test Question 2

The code for the method `deleteLink` is:

```
public void deleteLink(Object vertex1, Object vertex2)
{
int index1, index2;
index1 = ((Integer)nodeNames.get(vertex1)).intValue();
index2 = ((Integer)nodeNames.get(vertex2)).intValue();
links[index1][index2] = links[index2][index1] = false;
}
```

First, it finds the index of the two objects whose link is to be deleted. It then deletes the entries associated with these objects by setting the entries to false. Notice that since the class does not carry out any error processing there is no check on whether the objects are, in fact, part of the graph.

Self Test Question 3

The code for the method is shown below:

```
public int degree(Object vertex)
{
int index, count=0;
index = ((Integer)nodeNames.get(vertex)).intValue();
for(int j = 0;j<size;j++)
   if(links[index][j])
      count++;
return count;
}
```

It first finds the index of the argument in the array and then loops down it counting the number of true values in the links array row; since the array is symmetric it could have processed the corresponding column.

Self Test Question 4

Yes, it would require some modification. You would need some way of keeping track of the number of each vertex which has been deleted. addVertex would also need to be changed. At present it assumes that the next vertex number will equal the number of vertices. If deletion was allowed, it would first have to look for some vertex numbers corresponding to deleted vertices before assuming this. If there were no deletions then the next vertex number would be the number of vertices; if there was, however, at least one deletion then the number would correspond to the number of one of the deleted vertices.

Self Test Question 5

The criticism is that there is some duplication of data. The instance variable weights contains duplicates of the edges within edges.

Self Test Question 6

hashCode is required since edges are going to be stored in a HashMap object and the class requires this method to calculate a hash value. toString enables the vertex to be displayed and equals is also needed for the storage of edges in a HashMap since equality comparisons are to be carried out. hashCode is very simple: all it does is to return the hash code by calculating the sum of the two objects which make up the vertices.

Self Test Question 7

If what was required was for each vertex to be displayed on `System.out`, then all that would be needed is for a class to implement the interface and provide the code for `apply`. This is shown below:

```
public class Printer implements AppObjectProcess{

public void apply(Object o)
{
System.out.println("Visit "+o);
}

}
```

Then all that is required to display each of the vertices of a graph `g` would be the execution of the line of code

```
g.visitAndDo(new Printer())
```

Chapter 11

Self Test Question 1

Any of the strategies outlined in the earlier parts of the book could be used. For example, a binary search or a hashed search could be used.

Self Test Question 2

Figure A.1 shows the instantiation of the *Template* pattern in terms of the collections that we have described. Here `Collection` is the instantiation of `AbstractClass` and `LinearCollection` is the instantiation of `ConcreteClass`.

Self Test Question 3

The code is shown below:

```
TransformerExtendedPrintWriter cepw =
    new TransformerExtendedPrintWriter
        (new PrintWriter(System.out,true),new
TwoCharCompressor());
```

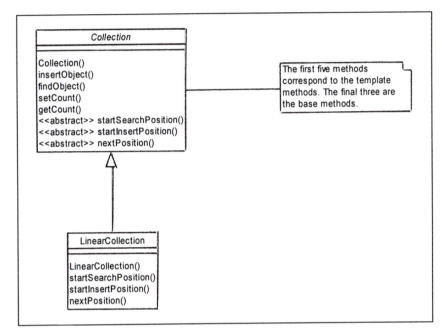

Figure A.1
The solution
to self test
question 2

This creates an object which is based on a PrintWriter that writes to the System.out stream and autoflushes (the role of the true-valued second argument) and to which the functionality in a TwoCharCompressor object is applied. This object, which is based on a class which subclasses Transformer, carries out a simple compression of the text by replacing frequent pairs of characters with a single character resulting in a compressed text.

Chapter 12

Self Test Question 1

It has the advantage that an *explicit* attempt to add a child to a leaf would be quickly caught at compile time, since a leaf class would then not have any child administration methods such as addComponent. However, there is a price to pay for this: you lose transparency because similar classes will have different interfaces[1]. This means that if you were manipulating objects defined by Component you would need to carry out some check on the object before using a method which might not be defined for that class. For example, if the array compArray contained Component objects which could be defined by the subclasses of Component: Leaf and Composite, then code such as:

```
//Code to carry out manipulation of children
```

---

[1] In this book I use the term *interface* of a class to denote the list methods associated with a class.

```
if (compArray[i] instanceof  Composite)
    //Carry out child processing
else
    //Raise some error
```

This code is to be frowned upon as it reverts to a style of procedural programming which object-oriented technology aims to overcome.

Index